God, Sex & the Search for Lost Wonder

Mike Starkey

InterVarsity Press
Downers Grove, Illinois

InterVarsity Press
P.O. Box 1400, Downers Grove, IL 60515
World Wide Web: www.ivpress.com
E-mail: mail@ivpress.com

Second Edition: ©Mike Starkey 1998
First Edition: ©Mike Starkey 1997

*Published in the United States of America by InterVarsity Press, Downers Grove, Illinois, with
permission from SPCK, London. First published in Great Britain in 1997 under the title* God, Sex and
Generation X.

InterVarsity Press® *is the book-publishing division of InterVarsity Christian Fellowship/USA*®, *a
student movement active on campus at hundreds of universities, colleges and schools of nursing in the
United States of America, and a member movement of the International Fellowship of Evangelical
Students. For information about local and regional activities, write Public Relations Dept.,
InterVarsity Christian Fellowship/USA, 6400 Schroeder Rd., P.O. Box 7895, Madison, WI 53707-7895.*

All Scripture quotations, unless otherwise indicated, are taken from the Holy Bible, New International
Version®. NIV®. *Copyright ©1973, 1978, 1984 by International Bible Society. Used by permission of
Zondervan Publishing House. All rights reserved.*

Cover illustration: Dave Zentner

ISBN 0-8308-1937-1

Printed in the United States of America ♻

Library of Congress Cataloging-in-Publication Data

Starkey, Mike.
    [God, sex, and generation X]
    *God, sex & the search for lost wonder : for those looking for
something to believe in / Mike Starkey.*
        p.   cm.
    *Originally published: God, sex and generation X. London:
SPCK, 1997.*
    Includes bibliographical references.
    ISBN 0-8308-1937-1 (alk. paper)
    *1. Sex—Religious aspects—Christianity.   2. Generation X.
3. Apologetics.   I. Title.*
    BT708.S83   1998
    241'.66—dc21   97-32987
                                                            CIP

19	18	17	16	15	14	13	12	11	10	9	8	7	6	5	4	3	2	1
14	13	12	11	10	09	08	07	06	05	04	03	02	01	00	99	98

for Naomi

1

The Awe in Ordinary

won•der n. 1. The feeling excited by something strange; a mixture of surprise, curiosity, and sometimes awe. 2. Something that causes such a feeling, such as a miracle.
Collins English Dictionary

*T*he first tentative hints of dawn were starting to appear in the dark sky. I gripped the wheel of the car and leaned forward, straining to see through the driving rain. I had my headlights on high, and my heart was pounding even faster and more violently than the frantic windshield wipers. I was late. Very late.

It was 5:30 a.m. We had stayed out till past midnight the previous night, a big mistake when you work the early shift, especially when your vocal newborn son robs you of your usual few short hours of badly needed sleep. By six o'clock I had to be in the small sound-proof booth, headphones on, fader up, with a calm voice that belied the chaos of both newsreader and newsroom as I announced, "CNFM News at six a.m."

In less than half an hour I had to achieve the impossible: finish the drive along the winding country lanes between our isolated cottage and the radio station on the edge of Cambridge; then unlock the station doors, make my way to the newsroom and check the overnight computer feed of stories from Independent Radio News in London; select and edit some twenty-second pieces of audio from the overnight automatic tape machine; call the local emergency services; follow up any local stories; write the local news; compose a three-minute bulletin of national, international and local news; and then be seated in the news booth, ready for the exact second when the long hand on the studio clock hits the vertical.

It would take a miracle. Or maybe just a little more speed. I pushed my foot down hard on the accelerator, confident that I could maneuver the car around each serpentine curve of the roads I knew so well. But I had underestimated the wet road, the dark sky, the blinding rain, the sheer fatigue that dulled my every reaction.

Suddenly I found myself speeding around a bend that seemed sharper than I had remembered. The car began an uncontrollable skid, wildly careening from one side of the road to the other.

I have never enjoyed roller coasters, but now I was on my very own white-knuckle ride, spinning out of control. I felt the car fly off the road over a deep drainage ditch and turn a somersault in midair. For those few seconds my sense of powerlessness was overwhelming. *O God,* I prayed, *help!*

That morning I did not read the news. I *was* the news. "CNFM News at seven. A CNFM reporter narrowly escaped death when his car skidded off a wet country road in the early hours of this morning . . ."

The car bounced upside down in a field, crushing the roof in toward me. Then it flew up in the air again and landed right side up, a mangled wreck of metal and earth.

All was uncannily still. I sat for a few moments, stunned, before I tried the door handle. To my surprise the door opened, and I fell out, too weak to stand. I ran—on unsteady legs—a mile or so to the nearest village, where my in-laws lived. I reached their house and pounded on their door, seeing the surprise and concern in their eyes when they finally appeared and realized who it was.

That morning I did not read the news. I *was* the news. "CNFM News at seven. A CNFM reporter narrowly escaped death when his car skidded off a wet country road in the early hours of this morning . . ."

I still have flashbacks to that accident. I remember clearly the numbing terror as the car slid back and forth on the wet road, how it felt to fly out of control, not knowing where I might land—even whether I would be alive when I did. This experience left me profoundly shaken, even years later. Having stared death in the face, I would never again view life through the same eyes.

Wonder and the Gift of Being

I could no longer take life for granted. The simple act of being had seemed the most inconsequential of feats, a dull precondition for the excitement of doing. Now existence itself was a miracle, an unexpected gift. That day in 1990 when I wrote off the car, and almost wrote myself out of the script of life, something in my attitude toward the everyday shifted, fundamentally and irreversibly. I became struck by the obviousness that everything out there—stones, trees, houses, discarded pieces of chewing gum —might not have been. Existence is not a given. It is a gift.

The most commonplace began to appear new and strange. While before I was faced with the trivial and banal, now I began to sense the surprise, curiosity and awe that together produce wonder.

Oddly, the mere idea that something was there as opposed to not there became striking to me. I was experiencing the world as a wonderful place.

The word *is* should make children marvel, bank tellers and window cleaners skip, retirees throw their hats into the air, because it is the opposite of *isn't*. By some gratuitous miracle the wide, gray domains of *isn't* have been invaded by the joyful presence of a wild, cheery *is*. With every *is* the realms of nonbeing have once again been ravaged by something alien. Something has hovered over waste and void and has spoken existence into being. And the least we can do each morning is shout a heartfelt "Thanks!"

Like Damocles' sword, life itself hangs by a slender thread. It is only when the sword falls or threatens to fall that we appreciate the delicacy, strength and beauty of the thread that has held it.

One of the paradoxes of life is that we most fully appreciate something when its absence looms or becomes reality. That which was trite leaves a gaping hole when it is gone. The book, CD or gardening tool might stand untouched for years, but when we give it away it instantly becomes the very thing necessary for survival. Our favorite radio station becomes highly desirable when we are traveling outside our own country. "My mother had one, but she gave it away" is the dismal call of the penitent.

The art of wonder is the lost art of astonishment. Wonder is an attitude toward life and creation that takes nothing for granted, that knows that each molecule might not have been there given different circumstances. Wonder is treasuring the miraculous in the mundane. It is refusing to take for granted even the most prosaic aspects of the daily grind. It is rediscovering the bright twinkle on the things whose sheen has been dulled by familiarity.

Wonder is rediscovering people. Under its benevolence we are urged to focus not so much on the routine irritation of mislaid slippers as on the elaborate piece of functional art that is the human foot. Wonder is encountering those around us with open-mouthed surprise, as if they were the most eccentric strangers we had ever met. It is telling those closest to us all the sentimental, loving things we will one day put in their funeral eulogy. With wonder the catch is to do it while they are still alive.

••

Wonder is an attitude toward life and creation that takes nothing for granted, that knows that each molecule might not have been there given different circumstances.

••

Wonder is gratitude for the fat, chuckling *is* that constitutes our earthly existence, an amazement that takes nothing for granted.

Queen Victoria's Generation X

In 1892 an eighteen-year-old student named Gilbert Keith Chesterton began his studies at the Slade School of Art in London. His time at the Slade coincided with a period of intense inner turmoil, a state aggravated by the spirit of the age in which he was living.

Some people imagine the Victorian era as a time of stern religious absolutes and prim moralizing, but this is far from what it really was like. By the 1890s Chesterton's generation was swimming in a tide of end-of-century decadence and intellectual cynicism, an atmosphere that profoundly influenced the young art student.

The bohemian Chesterton, like so many of his contemporaries, took potshots at religious dogma of any kind and reserved particular scorn for the clergy, who seemed to do little more than play power games.

Alongside Chesterton's religious cynicism was an attitude of skepticism toward life and the outside world, an adolescent sense that he alone was the center of the universe and that without his own mind it might all prove to be an illusion. Did the natural world exist outside his own imagining? Did other people have any objective existence aside from his perceptions of them? This attitude of philosophical skepticism would anticipate much of the thinking of the late twentieth century.

His creed was a kind of romantic humanism: having no need for God, humanity would manage to forge its own way to a glorious future. Humankind alone is divine, and all superstitions, dogmas and myths are no more than projections of our own desires onto the canvas of the universe.

As he was to note in later life, however, once a person stops believing in God, he does not believe in nothing—he believes in anything. And Chesterton was fascinated by the macabre and occult. His notebooks from this time are haunted by drawings of goblins and devils, their crooked grins testifying to his obsession with evil. His rejection of an earlier Victorian religiosity led to a dabbling with spiritualism and Ouija boards. He also appears to have been drawn, perhaps unconsciously, to the lurid and masochistic side of sex. His earlier school notebooks show doodles of people with hands tied behind their backs and naked figures being whipped. His imagination ran riot.

The mindset of this art student at the close of the nineteenth century sounds curiously familiar a hundred years later: a dying century; dissatisfaction with the fading dreams of an earlier generation; mistrust of institutional religion; belief that truth claims are little more than power games; fascination with decadence; romantic glorification of suicide; experimentation with occult and Eastern mysticisms (the late nineteenth century saw the first big turn toward the East in the search for spiritual enlightenment); attraction to the violent side of sexuality; loneliness; rising drug use; relishing anything that promised to titillate a jaded palate.

And yet it was an age profoundly searching for meaning, hope and intimacy, longing for truth, for relationships, for God. We have been here before. Chesterton and his turbulent days as a student closely parallel today's generation in their teens and twenties, a product of our own turmoil, as we will explore.

Light in the Tunnel

By the end of his time at the Slade in 1895, Chesterton began undergoing a profound philosophical shift, so much so that in later life he looked back on his student days as a time of darkness, even madness. In his *Autobiography* he records how he had felt himself "plunging deeper and deeper as in a blind spiritual suicide."[1]

What brought about this change? One factor seems to have been experiencing close, intimate relationships with other people. A fascination with evil is often sparked by the loneliness and isolation of adolescence. So it was with Chesterton.

As he entered his twenties he renewed old boyhood friendships, including his acquaintance with the writer E. C. Bentley, and through this friendship seems to have come a clearer vision of goodness and the virtues of trust and loyalty. Being open to another human being pulled

> Chesterton was fascinated by the macabre and occult. His notebooks from this time are haunted by drawings of goblins and devils, their crooked grins testifying to his obsession with evil.

Chesterton beyond the morbid confines of his own mind, a liberation for which he was profoundly grateful.

At the same time he increasingly realized that the forbidden lure of the black arts failed to come up with the goods. In his *Autobiography* he recalls how sessions with the Ouija board at that time would leave him not with secret powers and spiritual insight but with an aching head and a bad taste in his mouth, or—as he put it—"a bad smell in the mind."[2] Disillusioned and sickened by the occult, he was becoming more and more open to a new, positive vision of the world around him.

One place he found this was the writings of the poet Walt Whitman. While reading Whitman he encountered a zest for life, a slap in the face of decadence and pessimism, and a sense of the dignity and nobility of humankind. Gradually he became more cynical toward the fashionable cynicism of his day. He began to doubt his own doubting and grew bored with boredom.

All this time Chesterton had not yet begun to seriously reconsider the orthodox Christianity dumped by his contemporaries. That was to begin the following year when he met his wife-to-be, Frances, a practicing Christian. All he knew now was that he had become skeptical of skepticism, indifferent to moral indifference, and was becoming an increasingly intrigued reader of the Bible.

By the age of twenty-one, as he began work in the publishing world, he found himself newly fascinated by the wonder of the humdrum. He was rediscovering a sense of astonishment at the mundane and was bursting with gratitude for the sheer gift of life. Before long the missing piece of the puzzle would be put into place. He would find that the gratitude welling up inside him was the natural, instinctive response of the recipient to the giver, the response of a creature to its Creator.

He was awaking to wonder. His great, good-humored sanity, which was to characterize his life and work, was stirred through a renewal of wonder in relationships with other people, a renewal of wonder at the earth, and the first inklings of a wonder toward God.

Home Is a Strange Land

Toward the end of his time at the Slade, as he was beginning to cast off his fashionable morbidity and skepticism, Chesterton wrote a short story entitled "Homesick at Home."[3] It tells of a man called White Wynd who had been born, raised, married and raised a family in the same white farmhouse by a river. One day the man becomes angry, restless and—paradoxically—stricken with homesickness. He longs for home, even though he has never once left his own farmhouse.

Despite the entreaties of his family, he sets out around the world to discover the excitement of new horizons. After countless adventures he reaches the very end of the world, and it dawns on him that the place he has reached is the white farmhouse by the river, his own wife, his own children. It is the most beautiful place he has ever seen. He has returned home and seen the familiar with new eyes, and it will never be the same again.

The story charts Chesterton's own realization of how sheer habit can dull our astonishment at that which is ours. The most miraculous place we will ever go is home, seeing it as if for the first time. But to realize this, most of us need to lose it for a while, or at least lose our grip on it.

Chesterton's parable suggests that the shortest way home might be to go around the world and see the familiar through new eyes. "Homesick at Home" is Chesterton's own story, the drama of someone escaping from lethargy and decadence to rediscover the wonder of the commonplace. This sense of wonder at the everyday runs like a silver thread through Chesterton's poems, plays, novels and journalism, until his death in 1936.

In a collection of essays from 1905, *Heretics,* Chesterton offers an example of how we can become desensitized to wonder by overfamiliarity. He tells how an editor at a publishing company where he was working entered the room, wielding a book titled *Mr. Smith* or *The Smith Family* and cynically observing that a book with such a title could harbor nothing of the mysterious or romantic.

Chesterton, in reply, points out that, on the contrary, "in the case of Smith, the name is so poetical that it must be an arduous and heroic matter for the man to live up to it. The brute repose of Nature, the passionate cunning of man, the strongest of earthly metals, the weirdest of earthly elements, the unconquerable iron subdued by its only conqueror, the wheel and plowshare, the sword and steam hammer, the arraying of armies and the whole legend of arms, all these things are written, briefly indeed, but quite legibly, on the visiting-card of Mr. Smith."[4]

He reminds us that any perceived dullness lies not in the name of Smith, "this name made of iron and flame," but in the dullness of our own minds, the dullness of eyes that can no longer see the sparks and the clash of metal.

Perhaps Chesterton's greatest and most enduring work is his rousing 1908 defense of Christianity against its cultured despisers, *Orthodoxy*. In the second paragraph of the book he writes that he has long fancied writing a novel about a yachtsman who miscalculated his course and "discovered" England, thinking it was some new island in the South Seas.

He says that he himself is that yachtsman. He had allowed his imagination to set sail into wild, fantastic regions, deep with mystery and color. He set out to encounter the new and exotic, only to find that he arrived at the shores of historic Christianity and discovered that it was indeed a strange country.

In *Orthodoxy* Chesterton applies the experience of White Wynd to the whole human race, a people whose familiarity with revealed religion has obscured its restless passion and beauty. We will not appreciate the beauty and scandal of historic Christianity, he claims, until a jaded culture learns to see it as if for the first time.

The plump English journalist who set sail for exotic, uncharted regions, only to discover that home itself is a strange land, is the poet laureate of wonder. Chesterton, escapee from Queen Victoria's blank generation, is the sort of prophet desperately wanted by a new generation for whom life has lost its sparkle, a culture that has lost its appetite. He is the kind of doctor urgently needed by a generation that wakes up only to discover that its sense of wonder has been surgically removed.

Our Own Loss of Wonder

The rest of this book charts the conviction that there has been an unparalleled loss of wonder among today's young adults, the generation widely known as baby busters or Generation X. The bulk of the

> He had allowed his imagination to set sail into wild, fantastic regions, deep with mystery and color. He set out to encounter the new and exotic.

book attempts to account for this generation's loss of wonder in three key areas: relationships, attitudes toward the world around us and attitudes toward God.

It was, significantly, the reawakening of wonder in precisely these areas that shook Chesterton from his end-of-the-century daze. The claim of this book is that the promise of a reawakened sense of wonder in these same three areas holds out a vision of hope to a generation so different from Chesterton's—and yet so alike—some one hundred years later.

2

Sex: The Lost Wonder
of Intimacy

●●●

**There is no better way to dismantle a personality
than to isolate it.**
Diana, Princess of Wales,
BBC TV's *Panorama* (1995)

*O*ne of the paradoxes of our sex-obsessed culture is that we
have achieved something our Puritan and Victorian forebears never
even considered a possibility: we have made sex boring.

Our culture deals with sex the way chocolate manufacturers deal
with clandestine snacking by employees. Instead of banning workers from sneaking chocolate bars, companies encourage them to
indulge. For about two weeks the delighted workers eat as much
chocolate as they can. Soon, however, they begin to feel nauseated.
As the months go by chocolate is no longer a forbidden temptation
but something trite, a matter of supreme indifference.

The Death of Sex: Some Snapshots
For several weeks I worked at a youth club in a small town in
northern England. As I sat with the group of fourteen- to
eighteen-year-olds on the ripped chairs with our cans of Coke, they

joked about who'd been "shagging" (having sex with) whom recently. Johnny shagged Tracy, who had also been shagging Dave. Kelly had been shagging Nev, and Kev and Mick had been shagging quite a few girls too. Shagging was an alternative to bowling or movies. It kept you from getting quite so bored.

One year I attended a Christian conference held annually at a British resort center. I got talking to one of the girls who were working at the center for the vacation season. She told me how every week a minibus came to take large numbers of the teenage staff to the "clap clinic" in town. Working at that resort offered lots of opportunities for casual sexual encounters with people you might never meet again, as well as many chances to contract gonorrhea or other sexually transmitted diseases. And the medical profession picked up the pieces.

Every year thousands of young adults fly to resorts for under-thirties' vacations whose publicity scarcely disguises that the whole point is sun, sea and sex, with the emphasis on the sex. In my days as a radio journalist, a young colleague told me tales of her own encounter with the leading company behind such vacations. One concerned the nightly "games" in a resort, which involved throwing your room keys into a pile and then performing a "lucky dip" to see whose bed you would share that night. If you ended up with somebody who made you feel physically sick, too bad. Better luck the following night.

Every weekday the advertising-based paper *Loot* hits the news stands of London. Hundreds of ads in the "personal" section are requests couched in a range of creative euphemisms: "For adult fun and friendship," "In need of excitement," "Fun nights in," "Adventurous male required," "Broadminded couples only." Sex is advertised and requested in the same way as a secondhand lawn mower. These requests for sex outnumber the ads in the "friendship" section several dozen to one, and many are from married couples. Their ads seek out other couples, and various combinations of people, to join them for casual sex.

Behind each ad lies human tragedy, the tragedy of people made for relational intimacy and vulnerability, now reduced to trawling the lowlife of the city for an

> One nightly "game" in a resort involved throwing your room keys into a pile and then performing a "lucky dip" to see whose bed you would share that night.

ever more extreme sexual fix. It is the tragedy of people who have persuaded themselves that faithful intimacy with one partner is dull, so they need to keep pushing back the frontiers of weirdness to approach the thrill they once derived from sex. In order to get their fix such people run enormous risks of disease, violence, blackmail and rape, not to mention many unseen emotional consequences.

I recently watched a leading relational counselor being interviewed on TV. She was asked what her advice for young people was in the area of sexual relationships. After a moment's thought, she offered: "Sex is better if you like the person you're sleeping with."

Most of my contemporaries no longer make love. They shag, bonk and screw—quickly, anonymously, lovelessly. The generation searching for intimacy more pitifully than any other in history has taken the central sacrament of interpersonal intimacy and killed it dead. We have the dubious privilege of living in the culture that is presiding over the death of eroticism.

Ours is a culture crying out for intimacy, but able to conceive of accessing it only through sex. So desperate were we for intimacy that we ripped the veil off sexuality, exposed myriad hidden things to public gaze and indulged to excess. But now we find that somebody somewhere along the line was not telling us the truth.

Somebody we trusted sent us down a blind alley, and we found ourselves robbed of the little intimacy we still had.

The Death of Sex: Who Pulled the Trigger?

What went wrong in our view of sex? At first glance it might look as if Generation X is to blame for the death of sex, with its casual, "fast-food" approach to sexuality and its fear of commitment. On closer inspection, however, it becomes clear that Xers are attempting to resuscitate a corpse that was finished off by somebody else. And a number of older figures can be glimpsed guiltily skulking in the distance. This group includes economists, sixties permissives, modern marketers, even some Christian clerics. And a suspiciously large number of them appear to be baby boomers.

Individualism, or me-first-ism, is not a new phenomenon. It has been a central pillar of European thought since the sixteenth century, and by the eighteenth century it had become the underlying mindset of our culture.

The high-water mark of individualism was in the postwar years, the era of the baby boom, and reached its climax in the Reagan eighties. The watchword of an entire culture became personal freedom: freedom of choice, freedom to own, freedom to earn and to succeed. The economic theories of Adam Smith (1723-1790), which emphasized progress through self-interest, became enshrined at the heart of the burgeoning creed of capitalism: as individuals pursue their own well-being, they somehow help the well-being of society.

Experts differ over whether the theory works in the field of economics. But one thing is beyond doubt: the attitude claiming that I am an autonomous individual with a right to pursue my personal goals and insist on personal freedoms has stuck. Individualism is not rooted in Christianity, as many suspect. Rather it marks a full-scale denial of the Christian view that I am essentially a person in relationship. Individualism claims that I find myself in myself by digging inside my own solitary brain, by pursuing my own solitary goals.

The underlying individualism of our culture has profoundly colored the way we view the whole of life, including sex—before, during and after marriage.

If personal freedom is the supreme value, then traditional limitations on sexuality could be viewed only negatively by the permissives of the sixties. Yet there is no earthly reason that in a sane society constraints should be seen as negative. The constraint of a lifejacket keeps us afloat. The constraint of walls keeps in heat and keeps out burglars. But when contraception and abortion became widely available in the 1960s, few young adults stopped to ask if the walls so carefully built around sexuality for centuries might in fact have been protective walls. All that mattered was that they were constraints, and constraints were bad. Any limitations had to be a blasphemy against the hallowed idol of personal freedom.

Despite the growing emphasis on individual liberty, until the sixties one compelling reason to exercise sexual restraint was still in place: the risk of pregnancy. But with contraception and abortion, that risk was largely done away with. The shift in the practice of sex outside a permanent, committed relationship was dramatic.

American teenagers in the early 1970s were twice as likely to have had sexual intercourse as their counterparts in the early 1960s. The rates of sexual activity for American fifteen- to nineteen-year-olds increased 45 percent between 1970 and 1980 and increased another 20 percent in the short period between 1985 and 1988.[1] By 1990, 32 percent of girls ages fourteen and fifteen and 49 percent of boys the same age had had sex.[2] And today over half of unmarried girls and 60 percent of unmarried boys between the ages of fifteen and nineteen have had sexual intercourse at least once.[3]

In the space of not much more than a decade, sex shifted from the category of delayed gratification to instant gratification. At a stroke, wonder died, because, unknown to the moral anarchists of the sixties, the walls they had so gleefully kicked down did have a purpose: to preserve wonder. It was to keep sex special, to keep it as something to be anticipated with bated breath.

The effects of the sixties' libertarian revolution were a little like bludgeoning Santa Claus to death in order to get at the presents immediately—an act of impatience that ruins the whole point of the tradition and spoils the fun for everybody. But the issue was presented as one of personal freedom, that pied piper who must be followed wherever he might lead. And in the case of baby boomers, he led directly to divorce court.

The Tragic Fallout

In 1970 California was the first state to adopt no-fault divorce, making it much easier for couples to obtain a divorce by not having to assign blame to either party. This practice was later adopted nationwide, and Americans soon saw the divorce rate shooting sky-high. By the early 1980s divorce seemed almost out of control, with one out of every two marriages failing, a statistic that has more or less stayed the same to the present.[4] The U.S. currently has the highest divorce rate in the world,[5] and almost half of all Xers come from broken homes.

Crude generalizations about people's lives are dangerous. Divorce is rarely something undertaken glibly and is frequently the result of extreme pressures on a couple from outside—often due to factors such as money and housing. But one thing still needs to be stated clearly: the high divorce rate is in large part due to our culture's uncritical bowing before the idol of personal freedom. To the boomer, personal goals come first and people come second. People are more a means to an end than an end in themselves. The attitude that spawned the sixties' permissive society—what matters most is my personal fulfillment, my freedom to choose, my "rights"—has been carried over into marriage.

Marriage has been redefined in the popular mind from something that obligates me to another person to something that meets my emotional and sexual "needs." Vows have been subtly changed from a binding covenant to an optimistic ideal. It is increasingly taken for granted that "for better or for worse" means "for as long as you bring me satisfaction, and unless I find somebody better."

This might sound like an exaggeration and an unduly harsh judgment. But it is an attitude—expressed in different ways—that I regularly hear voiced by countless young adults. Not least is it reflected in their increasing reluctance to take on the

> The effects of the sixties' libertarian revolution were a little like bludgeoning Santa Claus to death in order to get at the presents immediately—an act of impatience that ruins the whole point of the tradition and spoils the fun for everybody.

commitments of marriage at all. By 1988 there were 2.3 million unmarried cohabiting couples,[6] a figure most likely even higher today.

In such a climate people will go to great lengths to avoid blaming themselves for problems in marriage. If I am ultimately the center of my own concerns, it follows that I will defend my corner and assert my own rightness. To this end our culture has latched on to the idea of "incompatibility" between partners. This passes the blame for relationship breakdown from ourselves to some basic flaw in the marriage. The catastrophic result is that, faced with antagonism in a relationship, we tend not to confront our own failings but to end the marriage, claiming it is beyond repair.

Time and again I have seen people abandon one marriage and

soon after start another, without ever asking what it was in themselves that might have contributed to the ending of the first. Sure enough, the same patterns of behavior reappear in the second, the third and so on. Individualism whispers that we are never to blame, that we can always pass the buck, and it discourages us from addressing our own destructive tendencies and shortcomings.

Commitment to relationships is on the decline, and yet, in a culture that has opened Pandora's box of condoms, sex is everywhere. In one short journey from my home in north London to the city center, I walk past several hundred overt images and messages of sexuality on magazine racks, on billboards, on posters in the subway, in newspapers, in shop windows, on T-shirts, on commercial radio. Even the children's slide in the park near our home is sometimes decorated with used contraceptives. Urban and suburban life in the West whispers, shouts and screams sex almost incessantly. The inheritance of Xers is to live lives emotionally numbed but sexually aroused.

We have a generation pulling back from vulnerability, a generation that has learned emotional numbness as a strategy of survival and is afraid of long-term commitment. It is a generation relationally stunted but at the same time sexually sated, that on both counts—emotional and sexual—has lost the wonder of personal intimacy. Young adults have pushed personal relationships to the top of the agenda, yet our culture can offer only more individualism and more commitment-free sex. The downward spiral accelerates.

We need a radically new vision of relational intimacy, one that attacks the whole charade at its very roots. Such a vision is offered by a Christianity that is fundamentally relational, sexual, and that offers intimacy. It is this vision we will explore in chapters four and five. But the vision has been blurred and even obscured in churches that are afraid of the human body, for whom even talk of sex is taboo, and that see our embodied natures as somehow less ideal than disembodied souls.

••

We need a radically new vision of relational intimacy, one that attacks the whole charade at its very roots.

••

Some Christians realize that the attitudes embodied in such churches are not right, and they give up on them in disgust. They then opt for the only other options they think are available, the casual sexuality pushed by the media and assumed in much sex education. They rightly react against a system that seeks to suffocate the body and deny their God-given sexuality, but wrongly assume that this otherworldly, unbiblical religiosity represents the entire Christian understanding of sex.

Collateral Damage: The Death of Friendship

When the protective walls around sex are broken, this makes not only for bad morality but also for bad sex. But there is another victim trampled in the general stampede. Nonsexual intimacy between the sexes has particularly suffered. Many women my age choose gay men as their closest male friends. One of these women, Mary, explained why:

With most men there's this sense that you know what they're after. Everything is all about working toward sex. So if they're nice to you or take you out, it's because they want to get you into bed. For most of them it's as if having sex is just a way of saying, "Thanks for a nice evening." Sometimes you just lie there and put up with it to get rid of them, and you fake orgasm earlier to get rid of them quicker.

But with Dan it's different. Because he's gay we both know

there's no possibility of sex. So he's just a really good friend, somebody I can talk to about everything, somebody who understands the real me and isn't just after a grope at the end of an evening.

Christian author Michele Guinness edited an anthology of writings on male-female relationships titled *Made for Each Other.* In her introduction to the section on friendship between men and women, she comments that this particular chapter is the shortest in the book because it was so hard to find anybody to write on the subject. People in our culture have had frighteningly little experience of nonerotic friendship across the genders.

Canadian writer Ronald Rolheiser makes the same sad observation: "Most people have given up on the ideal of deep life-giving friendships between women and men. . . . It is rare. Deep, intimate, chaste heterosexual friendship is no small achievement. We lack for models and are virtual pioneers in this partially uncharted area."

The art of nonsexual intimacy in the West is almost dead, although close friendships with people of the same sex and the opposite sex provide glimpses of the wonder for which intimacy was created. But for most Xers the wonder has been drained from all relationships. Friendships are failing because affection is treated as little more than foreplay, and sex is failing because it is something routine and banal.

3

The Loss of the Sacred in the Sexual

••

Awake, north wind, and come, south wind!
Blow on my garden, that its fragrance may spread abroad.
Let my lover come into his garden and taste its choice fruits.
Song of Songs 4:16

*I*f sex has been made boring, and if friendship has died, is it any wonder that we have also lost the magical qualities of a man and woman becoming a mystical union? Other cultures and other eras considered sex a sacred act, almost religious in nature. But where is the sacred now?

We look for the sacred in many different places. Some look for it in friendship. But a culture raised to be defensive and to mistrust others finds it hard to lower the barriers far enough to show the vulnerability that life-affirming friendships are made of.

Others look for the sacred in serial sexual relationships, hoping against hope that the next one will bring the longed-for fulfillment. Still others try cohabitation, thinking that it will provide the stability of marriage without its finality.

Some people find the sacred more directly in religious cults and their promise of communal intimacy. Cults can easily capitalize on the rootlessness of young people who prize belonging above all else. To many young adults the sacrifice of minds and wallets is worthwhile if their hearts are nurtured by a caring community. A religiously illiterate culture that craves intimacy can be easily led by the emotions, even if told to believe blatant nonsense.

It is no surprise that the generation that has been denied the sexual parameters of the past should be desperately improvising parameters of its own. The most common of these improvised parameters become what is "normal." This is one reason for the phenomenal success of women's magazines and the recent wave of men's magazines with their endless reader surveys and opinion polls. In the absence of any lasting yardsticks, the only measure of the self is how I compare with what my contemporaries are up to: how many times a week, with how many partners, in how many positions, who's faking what and how often. The opinion survey is the only morality available to a generation soaked in postmodern relativism.

The big problem, however, is that we are a generation rebelling against our inheritance. The rampant, self-seeking ambition that characterizes boomers has caused untold damage to families, the environment and personal integrity. In this sense Xers are radicals, calling for a new ethic of cooperation, harmony and intimacy. Our relational vision marks a massive step forward in Western civilization. From a biblical perspective it is a vision far more compatible with the values of the gospel than the individualism of the past few decades—even the past few centuries.

But having the right ideals is one thing; making them a reality is quite another. The dilemma for Xers is that the only tools they have for building community and intimacy are those bequeathed to them by baby boomers: individualism, slogans about personal freedom, opinion polls and an aversion to absolutes. Xers' emotional numbing and distrust of others leave them with a void crying out to be filled by intimacy; but in a culture where sex is aggressively marketed, Xers believe they can fill their void only through sex. And casual sex poisons genuine friendship.

The Failure of Churches

An alternative vision of relationships as passionate and compassionate was being offered all along, as it had been for nearly two millennia. But those entrusted with being its guardians largely failed to communicate this vision.

Some theologians saw the revolutionaries smashing the protective walls of sexual intimacy and joined in the free-for-all. Not wanting to be thought old-fashioned, they glibly offered theological rationales for any new morality on the horizon. The liberal theology of the sixties and seventies can be seen as a faint halo drawn over baby boomer "me-centeredness." It was a

> We are a generation rebelling against our inheritance. The rampant, self-seeking ambition that characterizes boomers has caused untold damage to families, the environment and personal integrity.

large-scale abdication of integrity that many church leaders now find embarrassing.

There were those who during this period held on to a more biblical ideal, but they couched it so often in negatives and stern moralizing that anybody with any spark of life and spirit automatically rejected it wholesale. Many Xers know, to their detriment, how boring and unfulfilling casual sex may be, but at least it is not as bad as a dull church service.

Conservative churches have only themselves to blame for their failure to communicate a biblical vision for sex to postwar young adults. It takes quite a high degree of skill to make satisfying, wonder-filled sex and the possibility of intimate, committed friendship sound miserable, but that is precisely what many pastors, nuns and youth workers somehow achieved.

In their reaction against the sexual excesses of an individualistic culture, these Christians offered a disaster in its place. Some churches picked up on one particular antisex strand from church history and taught that the physicality of human beings and our capacity for sexuality are somehow wrong. This anti-body, anti-erotic stance would be laughable had its consequences not been so devastating.

The Bible says that God made the physical human body as the pinnacle of creation. God created embodied humanity in his own image and declared us "very good."[1] Part of God's original design for humanity was for us to be in relationship with each other, and an important way this can be expressed is through sex.

This needs to be underlined, since there is so much nonsense spoken about sex being a result of the first sin of humankind. That is completely untrue. The new creation was teeming with sexual activity long before it rebelled against the Creator. And this included animals ("God blessed them and said, 'Be fruitful and increase in number' "[2]) and humans ("God blessed them and said to them, 'Be fruitful and increase in number; fill the earth' "[3]).

God made man and woman for each other. In fact, the writer of Genesis tells us that God said, "It is not good for the man to be alone,"[4] and proceeded to create a woman to be a companion and helper for the man.

The Creator, whose motivation in creating people was love, has made us for love, a love that includes our sexuality. Often the antisex brigade has been led by a bad theology that splits the world into opposing poles of sacred and secular, physical and spiritual, elevating the one and despising the other. Such a distorted, bifocal perspective on the human body is completely unfaithful to historic

Christianity. It is bad enough that this bifocal Christianity has fundamentally misrepresented Christian teaching on sex and the human body. But the consequences for a generation losing its relational grip have been devastating.

Biblical faith affirms the goodness of the physical creation, the body and sexuality, and says we can find identity only in relationship. The Song of Songs in the Old Testament is an erotic poem full of explosive double-entendre. The heart of the Christian faith is the incarnation ("taking flesh") of God himself when Jesus became a human being. And the Christian vision of eternity includes the resurrection of the physical body.

Turning Inward, Turning Outward

In chapter one we looked at the young G. K. Chesterton living in the late nineteenth century. Here is another true story, this time about somebody at the end of the twentieth century. Dan, a student, is preoccupied with questions of identity: Who am I? Who is the real me? Why do I seem to be so different at home or with my friends or at college? Is there any solid "core" that is me at all? How do I find fulfillment in life?

Dan has been born into a culture that for at least the past two hundred years has told him that the answer to these questions lies in a stable, unchanging self that is his own and that he simply needs to discover. He is an individual whose academic and social education has trained him to stand on his own two feet, to be independent. The few bits of religious writing he has read also tell him to look for the answers within, digging into his own psyche.

So he digs and digs, but he cannot find a great deal. What is the point of looking for the answers within if there is nothing much there? So he sits in his dorm room, listening to his CDs, going deeper and deeper into his own mind, and begins to use nicotine and alcohol in an attempt to stimulate his jaded senses.

It is only when Dan eventually gets out of his room and joins some clubs and groups that things start to change. The paradox of Dan's situation is that it is when he is wrenched out of his own armchair and abandons the excavations into his own brain that he starts to find himself. He can come alive only when he finds himself in relationship with that which is other than himself.

Of Billiard Balls and Trees

This point can be illustrated diagrammatically. For several hundred years the West has worked on a billiard ball model of identity, which sees the self as a hard, enclosed ball that sometimes bounces off other balls: friends, neighbors, God and so on. The balls roll around on the green surface of the pool table until each is finally put into a pocket and leaves the game.

....

Little surprise, then, that it was the rediscovery of these three relationships—with others, with the earth and with God—that awoke G. K. Chesterton to wonder.

....

Every ball, on this model, is fundamentally separate but will occasionally touch other balls, even have its own course changed by them. The self, however, remains impregnable.

On the other hand, the biblical model is inescapably relational. The key relationships in which we participate are not simply other balls, knocking us in a particular direction. A wholly different picture is needed to convey what it is to be made in the image of God, a more organic image, such as a tree in a forest.

For a tree, independent, nonrelational existence is an impossibility. It must relate to the earth below for its water and nutrients and to the sky above for sunlight and oxygen. It is also in relationship with the vegetation around it. Each of the tree's relationships is in some sense dynamic and mutual. In the same way we too interact with and are substantially defined by our relationships with other people, with the world and with God.

The claim that we exist only in relationship should come as no surprise to anyone who takes the Christian story seriously. The Christian account denies that personality is an illusion (that the "true self" does not exist) and also denies that it is self-sufficient (that it finds the answers only within). Rather, every character is unique. Each is created by a loving Creator and has worth in his eyes. The self is stable, but not fixed or static; the only truly static people are corpses.

In fact, if we take seriously the Christian vision of one day living on a renewed earth, we will discover our "true" selves not so much by delving into our present psyche as by being oriented toward the future—what we are capable of becoming. The search for true identity urges us to journey. To be human is to be on the move.

As I relate to the world, I am unique because nobody else inhabits the same patch of earth as I do at this point in the story. Nobody else has traveled exactly the same path or has the same calling (vocation) as I. And I am unique as I relate to other people, because nobody else has the same network of relationships as I do.

Little surprise, then, that it was the rediscovery of these three relationships—with others, with the earth and with God—that awoke G. K. Chesterton to wonder. Together these three lead us into an encounter with something, or somebody, different from ourselves. They each open us up and make us vulnerable to that which is other. To be open to the otherness found in relating to others, the earth and God is to inhabit a world where reality constantly jumps out at us from behind a bush and surprises us.

To be human, according to the Christian story, is to root our identity in a dynamic interplay between other people, the earth and

God. It is to find joy and astonishment in these. It is to be open to wonder.

But if the wellsprings of wonder dry up, our identity will grow parched and wonder will evaporate. How to renew our wonder in intimacy is precisely the dilemma that the next two chapters will discuss.

4

A Radical Sexual Vision

●●●

**There are actually many females in the world, and some of them
are very beautiful. But where could I find again a face whose every
feature, even every wrinkle, is a reminder of the greatest and
sweetest memories of my life? Even my endless pains, my
irreplaceable losses, I read in your sweet countenance.**
Karl Marx, letter to his wife

*W*hat was trampled in the lemming-rush of 1960s liberalism?
Essentially it was the wisdom that sex is something so precious,
something so wonderful, that walls are needed to preserve the
wonder. And that these protective walls were there not to stop sex
from being fun and fulfilling, but precisely to guarantee that it is.

Some walls, such as the former Berlin Wall, are built to restrict
freedom and happiness. Other walls, such as those of a bank vault,
are to safeguard something precious. Still other walls, like the walls
of a house, are to protect small children against the wind, the rain
and those who would violate their vulnerability.

The sexual revolution of the sixties thought it was demolishing
a Berlin Wall, but it turns out to have been smashing vaults and
homes, leaving precious, vulnerable things undefended. We ought
to be furious with the older generation. But since these same
forebears bequeathed to us their worldview of individualism and

self-fulfillment—and since the guardians of a real alternative either threw in the towel or made their good news sound like bad news— little of an alternative vision has been offered.

But there is an alternative vision for sexuality and relationship, a radical, biblical vision that can be summarized in three statements:

☐ Alone I am incomplete.

☐ A partner is the subject, not an object.

☐ Real sex equals real commitment.

The first two points apply to both sexual and nonsexual relationships, and the third just to sexual ones. In a way each of these statements sounds innocuous, even obvious. But each in its own way is a bombshell for those reared with a limp, postsixties worldview. Taken together all three represent a radical, countercultural manifesto of sexuality for the third millennium, with roots planted deep in the wisdom of centuries.

Alone I Am Incomplete

The first point of our radical sexual vision is shared by both Christians and Xers. Together they affirm the essentially social nature of personhood. Both the Bible and the gut feelings of a numbed generation tell us that we are incapable of finding identity in isolation from other people. I am inescapably a being in relation.

> The 1980s celebrated the earning power of the individual, with British Prime Minister Margaret Thatcher denying that "society" even existed.

But to affirm this is to deny the philosophical base of Western culture for the past four hundred years. The philosopher René Descartes locked the West into radical individualism when he reflected that once everything else has been doubted, the one thing I cannot doubt is that I am an autonomous individual with my own mental processes:

"I think, therefore I am." The eighteenth-century Enlightenment celebrated the rational thought processes of the individual.

The eighteenth- and nineteenth-century Romantic movement celebrated the emotions of the isolated individual. (Jean-Jacques Rousseau, a precursor of Romanticism, wrote a book entitled *Reveries of the Solitary Walker* and gave up his own children to an orphanage.) The 1960s celebrated the sexual freedom of the individual and the power of the individual to forge his or her own destiny. The leading exponent of such thinking, existentialist writer Jean-Paul Sartre, grimly reflected that *"l'enfer, c'est les autres"*— hell is other people. The 1980s celebrated the earning power of the individual, with British Prime Minister Margaret Thatcher denying that "society" even existed.

Not since the Middle Ages has the West been dominated by a relational ideal, which says that people are inescapably bound together, that identity is essentially social. It took our pushing of individualism to the extremes of rampant consumerism, the death of sex, the loss of friendship, and the destruction of community and the earth before we realized that something was drastically wrong. It took all this before we finally began to take issue with the individualist cry that personal freedom should be valued above all else.

Xers are a generation that wants to break with this lonely, failed past. We value groups and communities rather than individuals. We reject the boomer lifestyle that says personal goals and ambitions are central and other people are primarily a means to achieving those ends. We have a greater sense of our place in an international community and enjoy the cultural diversity of "world music." We have a greater concern for marginal groups in society and see multiculturalism as normal.

We prize friendships, perhaps as an alternative to failed families. Even dating is done less in the manner of an older generation, by pairing off to the exclusion of others, than in larger groups with other friends. The experience of school has more to do with relationship than achievement—relationship with a peer group, but also with parents.

••

Love is patient, love is kind. It does not envy, it does not boast, it is not proud. It is not rude, it is not self-seeking, it is not easily angered, it keeps no record of wrongs.

••

We tend to reject the "ladder" model of careers in favor of jobs that foster relationships and help others. We are less concerned about achievement, but we know that for our parents' generation this is the primary goal. So we are anxious to achieve—not so much for ourselves as to please our parents.

The shift from individualism to relationship is an exciting vision, a colossal undertaking. But all the role models belong to the enemy camp! Even as we start to think about the restoration of community and relationship, the very patterns of thought by which we approach the issues are those handed on by the culture we despise. It is as if a pacifist is handed a machine gun and told to fight for his cause.

Where can we look to find solid support for these instincts? The answer lies in the only vigorous, viable tradition of the culture that is fundamentally relational: biblical Christianity, that good news which has so often been packaged to look like bad news.

The heart of the biblical vision for relationships is that we are not designed to be alone. It is alien to our nature to forge an identity alone, to live alone, to reflect alone, to worship alone, to work alone. People sometimes treat the statement "God is love" as though it were a meaningless cliché, but its implications are staggering. It means that the central, underlying principle of the universe is not survival, chaos or chance, but intimate relationship.

We were made from love and for love.

That is why the Bible offers examples of intense, committed, nonerotic friendship, including David (before he was king) and Jonathan (the son of King Saul), the widow Naomi and her daughter-in-law Ruth, the apostle Paul and his disciple Timothy, Jesus and his closest follower John. The instinct toward friendship and companionship is not icing on the cake of life—pleasant but ultimately unnecessary. It is the cake itself. The instinct toward all relationship, particularly with the opposite gender, is a yearning for wholeness. Without it we are incomplete.

In the book of Genesis we find the story of the builders of the tower of Babel, who aspired to be like gods. Their punishment was that their language—the vehicle of communication and intimacy—became confused. They couldn't understand each other. As a result their community scattered across the face of the earth.[1] In biblical terms, community is a blessing and the breakdown of community is a curse.

For this reason the Bible places a strong emphasis on getting love right. Paul's great poem of love in his first letter to the Christians in the ancient city of Corinth—a city well used to casual, loveless sex of every variety—gives us a wonderful picture of perfect love. First Corinthians 13 offers a checklist for real intimacy, after underlining the centrality of love:

> If I speak in the tongues of men and of angels, but have not love, I am only a resounding gong or a clanging cymbal. If I have the gift of prophecy and can fathom all mysteries and all knowledge, and if I have a faith that can move mountains, but have not love, I am nothing. If I give all I possess to the poor and surrender my body to the flames, but have not love, I gain nothing.
>
> Love is patient, love is kind. It does not envy, it does not boast, it is not proud. It is not rude, it is not self-seeking, it is not easily angered, it keeps no record of wrongs. Love does not delight in

evil but rejoices with the truth. It always protects, always trusts, always hopes, always perseveres.[2]

In this relational, biblical vision there is a particular role for the Christian church as a body of believers. In the Bible *church* refers not so much to buildings or liturgies as to people. And the particular calling of that body of people is to embody the love that is to bring hope, healing and intimacy to the world.

Our individualistic culture has taught us to view churchgoing as something a person chooses to do because it brings him or her personal satisfaction or personal meaning, an alternative to downhill skiing or stamp collecting. It is a lifestyle option. We live in a culture where baby boomers see nothing wrong with compulsive "church-shopping" to find the best "show" offered each week. This is far removed from the New Testament model of church as intimate commitment to a community of people.

Some churches express this in terms of sacrament—a concrete, visible embodiment of an invisible and spiritual reality. The definitive sacrament is Jesus of Nazareth, God in human flesh. The apostle Paul writes of the coming of Christ as a *mysterion*,[3] a Greek word that translates into Latin as *sacramentum*. Paul means that the sacrament of Christ is a mystery not in the sense of something hidden or unsolved, but in the sense that something hidden is being revealed. The loving character of God is seen and made real in the person of Jesus.

But after the death and resurrection of Christ, the sacrament of God's presence on earth is the church, because it constitutes the "body of Christ." Paul's reflections on love in 1 Corinthians 13 are better understood in the context of chapter 12 of the same letter, where he tells the young church that together they are a single body,[4] which is the body of Christ on earth.[5] If they take the body analogy seriously, they will realize that each part is vital for the working of the whole, that each has a distinct role to play in the functioning of the body.[6] There can be no such thing as a solitary believer. A person is a believer only insofar as he or she is a part of the sacramental body of Christ on earth, the body of people gripped by the gospel. And when Paul tells the same audience, "Don't you know that you yourselves are God's temple?"[7] the Greek for "you" is plural. It is together, not individually, that they constitute the holy sanctuary where God himself makes his home.

According to historic Christianity, the instincts of Xers are right: I am incomplete alone. Identity is relational, the basis of our survival and well-being is relational, and our faith is inescapably relational too.

A Partner Is the Subject, Not an Object

The fatal flaw in Western individualism has been in seeing each person as the sun at the center of his or her own solar system: alone, splendid, autonomous, but surrounded by a number of dependent planets.

This view shaped, and was in turn shaped by, many of the great thinkers and movements of the past two centuries, such as Charles Darwin, who gave rise to the belief that life is a struggle for individual survival, at the expense of others if necessary. Intimacy is merely a useful device for propagating one's own line.

The rise of postwar consumerism made us believe that only individual fulfillment mattered, that the goal of life was prosperity. That vision, referred to as the American dream, has urged on the aspirations of a now global culture.

Rampant individualism has shaped our attitudes, often unconsciously held, that say: "I am a subject. Other people are objects." People are of interest to me only as they contribute to my own goals of self-fulfillment and happiness. I relate in order to meet my emotional needs. I parent in order to express my parenting instinct. I have my rights to certain things, and others are there to help me achieve them. That which ought to undercut individualism—relationship—is co-opted into the service of personal autonomy.

The problem for Xers is that there is no other air to breathe. We inhale individualism simply by being alive. Once again, however, the assumptions of the culture are flatly contradicted by the Christian gospel, which brings us to the second point in our radical sexual vision—other people are not objects, defined only in relation to me. They are not there to meet my needs, bring me personal fulfillment or be my rivals in the battle for survival.

An encounter with another person is an encounter with something truly other than myself. That person has her own story, her own place in God's big story and her own network of defining relationships that bring her a stable, unique identity all her own. When we meet another person, befriend another person, make love to another person, our response should be one of astonishment and wonder at their sheer difference from ourselves.

In our society the main causes of relationship breakdown—taking people for granted, boredom, disagreements and physical violence—stem from the mistaken expectation that the real reason other people are around is to help us through life. Such an expectation is due to a lack of respect and awe of the other. It is only when we ditch this assumption that real, mutual relationship starts to become possible.

To love the world and be committed to the welfare of all people everywhere is easy. To love and be committed to one other person is the real test. We can swear our boundless devotion to the wellbeing of all humanity, but we do not have to put up with all humanity sitting at our dinner table, sleeping in our bed and leaving their socks under our sofa.

The idea of "humanity" is a product of our own creation—based on stereotypes, pictures and media reports. It is easy to love what is a projection of our own mind, that which we can control. But close friends or lovers demand more than just our benevolence. They demand intimacy, a meeting of two subjects in a context of mutual awe and respect.

Every intimate friendship and every expression of sexuality is a reenactment of the primal encounter of one human

> In our society the main causes of relationship breakdown—taking people for granted, boredom, disagreements and physical violence—stem from the mistaken expectation that the real reason other people are around is to help us through life.

subject with another. In male-female encounters we each stand in the same place as Adam and Eve. Canadian writer Mike Mason writes movingly in *The Mystery of Marriage* that this primary encounter with similarity-yet-otherness is at the heart of our sexuality.

For secretly we long to perpetuate that one astounding moment in the Garden of Eden. We long to stand in awe of one another, just as Adam and Eve must have done when they first locked gazes. We long for our whole body to tingle with the thrill of knowing that this one fascinating being, this being of a different gender, has been created especially for us and given to us unreservedly for our help, comfort and joy. Men and women ache for the heart with which to know this reality, and for the eyes with which to see one another (and therefore themselves) as the astounding miracles that they are.[8]

It is this crucial insight of intimacy as a meeting of awestruck equals that is behind Jesus' insistence that we should love each other as we love ourselves.[9] In a society of individuals, that is no easy task. It involves a degree of selflessness our culture has not prepared us for. Intimacy with another person might open me up to wholeness and satisfaction, but it could also open me up to pain and misunderstanding. The best part of intimacy, the "otherness" of the other, is also its most agonizing quality. Intimacy, that piquant blend of intense love and potential hurt, is challenging. But to fail to rise to the challenge is forever to accept second best.

Mike Mason says the central act of intimacy is contemplation: I gaze on another person, filled with wonder that something so similar to myself can at the same time be so impenetrably mysterious. I encounter the mystery of life beyond my own horizons. And as I engage intimately with another person, I contemplate the very image of God before my eyes.

Some claim that we are closer to God in a garden than anywhere else on earth, but in the mystery of human relationships we come closer to God than is possible in even the most sublime scene of natural beauty.

> We behave as if we could say with our naked bodies what we would not say with our mind, emotions or words.

In close friendship and in sexual intimacy two alien worlds meet and stare open-mouthed at each other, amazed to discover that they are not alone, amazed at finding intelligent life where none was expected.

Real Sex Equals Real Commitment

The previous two points of our radical sexual vision can be applied as much to friendship as to sexual relationships. Is there, then, no significant difference between the two? Does it follow that any relationship in which we find personal identity and wholeness, where there is genuine awe and wonder, should be expressed erotically? To answer this we need to look more closely at the meaning of sex itself.

Today's Western culture prides itself on being holistic, on integrating all the varied facets of the human makeup. The otherworldliness of Victorian piety or the rationalism of Enlightenment thought is not for us. Our culture believes it has rediscovered the physical body, the earth, spirituality, the power of the feminine and the insights of native cultures. And yet, in the area of sexuality, our culture is the least holistic that has ever existed. We have learned to live as if we could split the physical aspect of our makeup from the other aspects.

Body, mind and spirit belong together. To be holistic is to insist that all three dance in time, not letting one run off ahead of the rest. Postmodern thought rightly accuses the dominant Western intellectual traditions of allowing one aspect—mind—free rein while playing down the body. In the same way liberation theologians correctly accuse the dominant Western religious traditions of ignoring the radical challenge of Christianity to political and social structures.

But somehow sex is different. We behave as if we could say with our naked bodies what we would not say with our mind, emotions or words. Sexual intimacy says with the body: I love you, I give myself wholly to you, I am committed to you, I am exposing the deepest, most intimate parts of my very being to you, even as I expose the deepest, most intimate parts of my unclothed body to you.

This is not just something culturally relative, as if native peoples who wear very little walk around blasé about nakedness. Anthropologists will tell you that such people in fact have extremely sophisticated categories of dress and undress. The ways they express these categories are different from ours, certainly, and might involve little more than a slim thong around the waist, but they are very real nonetheless. We too instinctively know the difference between a person wearing a skimpy bathing suit and one lying totally naked on the beach, even though there may be little objective difference between the two.

The physical nakedness of sexual intimacy is about baring our soul to another person. It is about vulnerability and absolute surrender. It is about opening up the hidden, private areas of ourselves, both literally and metaphorically. Mason explains,

> Exposure of the body in a personal encounter is like the telling of one's deepest secret: afterwards there is no going back, no pretending that the secret is still one's own or that the other does not know. It is, in effect, the very last step in human relations, and therefore never one to be taken lightly. It is not a step that establishes deep intimacy, but one which presupposes it.[10]

In other words, sexual intercourse says, "This is absolute self-giving. I can give you no more of myself than this complete intimacy. This is the appropriate level of surrender because ours is a permanent, committed relationship." If Mason is right, and I believe he is, this has massive implications for a generation that reverses the process and, far from seeing sex as the ultimate point of intimacy, sees sex as a casual starting point that may or may not lead to intimacy.

One implication is that it diminishes our integrity as persons, since sex outside a context of trust and permanence—as in casual sex or adultery—is the art of telling lies. It is saying physically what one could never say in words: "I commit myself to you absolutely, permanently, vulnerably."

Another implication is that it downgrades the quality of sex. Experts tell us that good sex is not primarily about technique. It is about trust and openness, and it takes a very long time to get it right. Indeed, it takes years of embarrassment, mistakes and a context of good communication—and a sense of humor!—to get it right. All these factors are absent from casual sex. Time is short, communication minimal and trust nonexistent. All the preconditions of good sex are missing. We are raising a generation of bad lovers. Biblical

Christianity insists that sex needs to be protected by boundaries in part to maintain its quality.

Interestingly, surveys reveal that people in the West who have the most active sex lives, and have the highest rate of regular orgasms, are conservative Christians. An authoritative survey from 1994 of Americans' sex lives backs this up.[11] The researchers asked women whether they always experienced sexual climax during lovemaking. Of those who claimed no religious affiliation, 22 percent agreed that they did. The figure for conservative Protestant women was considerably higher, 32 percent. The study also found that conservative Protestant men and women lead all other groups, religious and nonreligious, in the frequency of sexual intercourse.

Christian sex has gotten bad press through the centuries. But an examination of history shows that sexually active conservative Protestants are no aberration. Their Puritan forebears, despite their largely undeserved reputation as world-deniers, wrote long and enthusiastically about sexuality and intimacy as divine blessings. Indeed, the Puritans' positive approach to sexuality was a cultural turning point for Western culture in that it overturned the earlier medieval glorification of celibacy. When one New England Puritan husband refused to have sex with his wife, their church excommunicated him.[12]

Another implication of seeing fast-food sex as the norm is an unlearning of the language of touch. When it becomes second nature to see touch as a precursor to sex, its subtlety is lost. The language of touch is almost as dead as Latin and Sanskrit. To a contemporary audience the novels of Jane Austen and early Hollywood movies might as well be products of another universe: seething passion expressed in the mere touch of a finger, a single kiss, the casual brush against a person's side.

Such novels and films speak with a vocabulary of touch most of us have never been taught. Only two options are open, especially for those of us with an Anglo-Saxon heritage: a complete absence of touch as we each defend our own private "space," or else full intercourse. It is as if we have learned a language in which the only means of expression are silence and screaming oneself hoarse.

Sex therapists tell us that the results of our illiteracy in the language of touch have been catastrophic for the quality of our lovemaking when it does occur, and that men are especially inept in this area. Sex therapists David Delvin and Christine Webber conducted a major sex survey in which they asked women to state the advice they would most like to give their male partners.[13] The overwhelming answer came back: "Tell them to take their time!" The authors also cite a survey of Scottish women that shows they would like a full hour of gentle touch before even thinking about climax. In a similar survey, women in the U.S. request between fifteen and forty-five minutes.

••

When we insist that sex is so precious it needs strong walls built around it, we say something about the wonder of intimacy that the fast-food sex junkies will never understand either.

••

Delvin and Webber quote the complaint of many women respondents: "My man touches and kisses me only when he wants sex." The message to women in such cases is clear: touch and kissing are only a prelude to the bedroom. The idea that these things might be ends in themselves, low-key expressions of affection, has largely been lost among men today.

Another implication of letting your body speak louder than your commitments is the loss of wonder in relationships. For years my wife and I had wanted to go out for the most spectacular meal imaginable—irrespective of cost—just to see what the experience would be like. Since our student days in Oxford we had driven wistfully past the entrance to the Manoir aux Quat' Saisons many times. The Manoir is the home of the internationally famous French chef Raymond Blanc, well known for turning eating into a fine art form.

After years of waiting and longing, I finally decided to take the plunge and secretly booked a table for two for my wife's birthday. The price of the meal was enough to make the strongest person go weak at the knees, but the combination of all the years of waiting and the exorbitant price made every tiny morsel a precious thing. Every mouthful was savored at length, every inch of the room's decor studied with appreciation.

Some will say we wasted our money or will tell me how many burgers and fries that money would have bought. But that would miss the point: there was something immeasurably precious and perfect about that evening. It said something about the wonder of fine cuisine, something fast-food devotees will never understand, and it said something about the wonder of my relationship with my wife.

When we insist that sex is so precious it needs strong walls built around it, we say something about the wonder of intimacy that the fast-food sex junkies will never understand either. They look on and actually feel sorry for us. They think that because we want to keep sex special, we are antisex. If it wasn't so tragic, the scale and the irony of their incomprehension would be rather funny.

5

The Wonder of Intimacy Renewed

●●●

Love is coming home.

Ronald Rolheiser, *Forgotten Among the Lilies*

*I*f we were to travel back in time to the ancient world and look for common points of reference, one of the cities where today's young adults would feel most at home would be the Greek city of Corinth. It was the commercial gateway between the thriving cultures of Italy and Asia, an economic boomtown with an international populace. Because of its cosmopolitan makeup it was a center where the culture, thinking and religions of the West mixed with mystery cults from the East. Its strategic position, commercialism and pluralism of cultures and creeds anticipated the multicultural cities of today such as London, New York, Los Angeles, Toronto and Sydney.

City of Casual Sex

We would have recognized much in the Corinthians' attitude toward sexuality. As a commercial seaport Corinth gained such a reputation for free and easy sex that the ancient writer Aristophanes used the term "act like a Corinthian" as a synonym for fornication. Many in Corinth saw sex as no more meaningful than a quick snack—a way of satisfying a bodily appetite, with no deeper significance.

••

Every act of sex is a declaration of covenant, a binding statement of commitment and surrender to that one special person.

••

The apostle Paul had friends in Corinth, and so it was natural that they should express the widespread view of their day about sex by quoting to him some of the popular sayings of their culture: "Everything is permissible for me," "Food for the stomach and the stomach for food." In other words, sex is what the body is there for. Let's get on and do it.

We know Paul's friends were quoting such sayings to him because in a letter he quotes these proverbs back at them before going on to offer his own thoughts on the issue.[1] In his reply Paul underlines a point that would have been familiar to anyone acquainted with the teachings of Jesus and Judaism, but quite alien to the lifestyle in Corinth. It is the idea that the act of sex makes two people into "one flesh."[2] This notion of one flesh goes back to the Genesis creation accounts:

The man said,
"This is now bone of my bones
    and flesh of my flesh;
she shall be called 'woman,'
    for she was taken out of man."
For this reason a man will leave his father and mother and
    be united to his wife, and they will become one flesh.[3]
The same image is underlined and reinforced by Jesus:

"Haven't you read," he replied, "that at the beginning the Creator 'made them male and female,' and said, 'For this reason a man will leave his father and mother and be united to his wife, and the two will become one flesh'? So they are no longer two, but one. Therefore what God has joined together, let man not separate."[4]

From Genesis to Paul via Jesus, the same message is given. We cannot split the language spoken by our bodies from the language spoken by our mouths. Sexual intercourse surrenders the body totally to one other person. It says, "This act is so utterly powerful to bind and unite that we are now no longer two but one."

According to the biblical story casual, commitment-free sex is a contradiction in terms. It simply cannot exist. Every act of sex is a declaration of covenant, a binding statement of commitment and surrender to that one special person. In the context of the Christian story, extramarital intercourse is in effect impossible, since by having sex you have already given the fullest statement of commitment and surrender anybody could ever give to another person.

This exclusive relationship lays the foundation for full sexual intimacy and is characterized by fidelity, trust, selflessness, permanence, surrender, affection and personal maturity. It is what we know as marriage, which is expressed in a vast range of cultural forms and family patterns.

The Subtlety of Marriage

The Christian vision insists that the norms of what we call marriage are not culturally bound but God-given and universal. And to stop short of the norms that characterize marriage is to stop short of a full commitment to permanence. It is only these norms that offer the rich, dark earth, the moisture and the sunlight that allow the bright, fragrant, delicate flower of sexuality to thrive.

I was brought up in a town near Stratford-upon-Avon, home of the great English playwright William Shakespeare and the Royal Shakespeare Company. One of the pleasures of life as a student was to arrive at the theater in Stratford on the evening of a performance and buy a cheap "student standby" ticket. This would allow impoverished enthusiasts such as myself to see the whole performance while standing up.

I would go, however, secure in the knowledge that by the intermission, and sometimes after just fifteen minutes, I would be seated in one of the best seats in the house. Such seats would be vacated by middle-aged American couples who would mutter as they left, "C'mon, honey, let's go check out a movie. This is just so boring."

In one sense they were right. A movie would give them all the culture and pathos a sound-bite culture can ask for. In another sense, however, their response was an admission of defeat. They had stopped short of a commitment to see things through to the end.

I was the last to complain; their loss was my gain. But I longed to tell them that there might be more to the arts than they had yet experienced, greater subtlety, poetry and nuance, that to stick with it might have helped resensitize them to the possibilities of great drama. Perhaps my ideals were unrealistic. Most people uncritically live out whatever their culture has given them, no matter how limited or impoverishing. But I still hold out the same vision for marriage. It is still possible.

> The reason the movie tells the wrong story is that the mistress is the most sane character in the film. She is the one who knows that the sexual encounter was more than recreational fun.

Our culture encourages us to reinterpret relationships in the same way that "greatest hits" compilations reinterpret classical music:

offering the highlights without the "boring" bits in between. The problem is that the highlights make sense only in the context of the long, seemingly uneventful stretches that join them. To want the highlights in isolation misses the very point of those highlights. We are denying ourselves the full glory, the full subtlety.

To speak of modern sexuality in such terms is not judgmentalism. I hope that no one, least of all Christians who believe in a gospel of God's unmerited, free blessings, would be judgmental of lifestyle options different from their own. There is no reason to single out falling short of a sexual ideal as being any different from falling short in other, less controversial areas, such as gossip, lack of charity, or judgmentalism itself. But it is a question of whether we live as optimistic visionaries or pessimistic realists.

Just Like the Movies

Fatal Attraction is an intensely powerful movie. Its problem, however, is that it tells the wrong story. It tells of a married man, played by Michael Douglas, who has a sexual fling with an unattached woman, played by Glenn Close. As far as the man is concerned, that is the end of it, but she has other ideas.

He attempts to return to normal family life as if nothing had happened, but she will not let it rest. The gory, repulsive ending of the film shows the man and his wife together killing the mistress, who by this stage has become like a crazed animal. Only then can they return to their domestic bliss.

The reason the movie tells the wrong story is that the mistress is the most sane character in the film. She is the one who knows that the sexual encounter was more than recreational fun. No sex can be casual, but here is a man who pretends it can be. Through sex he has spoken a depth of commitment he never for a moment considered keeping. The real story is left unexplored: the tragedy of a woman—her selfhood and her sexuality inseparable—who is the victim of a warped culture.

All this is why the heart of a biblical sexuality is a commitment to fidelity, which is an act of speech, will, body and feelings. This has implications not only for casual sex and adultery but also for whether a couple decides to stay together or separate.

As I was writing this book I learned of yet more of my acquaintances who are about to divorce. The reason given, as is so often, was that the partners were changing, "finding themselves" and growing away from each other. They needed to be free to be the people they "really" are, and their spouses had suddenly become a hindrance to that self-realization.

This is nonsense, based on the almost universally believed but totally wrong idea that we fundamentally "find ourselves" in isolation, by digging inside our own heads. It assumes that the "real" me is that autonomous individual who needs to get in touch with my own feelings, my own ambitions, my own priorities.

If we are right to say that we find our identity only in relationship with other people, it is doubly true that we can find ourselves only in the context of the binding commitments we have made to others, spouse and children alike. Simply to opt out is no solution. If my very self is inseparable from the relationships to which I belong, pulling away is not liberation. It is a partial suicide.

Rekindling the Wonder

In a culture that has lost its grip on intimacy, talking in the terms discussed in chapter four—alone I am incomplete; a partner is the subject, not an object; real sex equals real commitment—might sound wildly idealistic. What can we say to those whose experience is far removed from these ideals? Specifically, what about

☐ those people outside the lifelong committed relationship most cultures know as marriage?

☐ those people in a marriage that feels dry and lacking in all wonder?

☐ those who feel that their past experiences of casual sex have killed any possibility of wonder?

Let's look briefly at each.

Those Outside Marriage

We live in a culture that actively discourages personal integrity and maturity in relationships. Personal maturity involves learning the language of intimacy: when to whisper, when to shout, when to remain silent. Different registers are appropriate for different relationships.

When greeting most casual acquaintances a handshake is sufficient. For close friends—male and female—a warm hug and affectionate touch express that they are worth more than somebody we've just met. In a more exclusive partnership that stops short of total surrender and permanent commitment, it is right to begin with kissing, knowing that intercourse is simply not appropriate yet. Why should we learn to become skilled in the art of telling lies, especially to the one with whom we are learning intimacy and openness?

Many books about sexuality that are aimed at Christian teens give lists of dos and don'ts. This seems to miss the point and is in many ways counterproductive. For one thing, human nature is such that on seeing a list of prohibited pleasures, our immediate desire is to try out every single one of them! We ask what is so special about this thing that they are trying to keep us from doing. Second, it falls into the same trap as our sex-sated culture. It discourages maturity in relationships and personal responsibility. It lays down laws, telling what we ought to be doing, rather than inviting us to reflect on what will help us grow as integrated, fulfilled people and to discover the role one's sexual and other relationships play in the process of identity shaping.

So the message to those outside a lifetime covenant relationship is an invitation to intimacy and relationship, no less so than to those who are married. But the ways this is expressed will be different. It will involve rediscovering the lost art of vulnerable, self-giving friendship, with people of the opposite sex and the same sex, and rediscovering the touch of affection. Most of all it will involve learning to be a whole, integrated person, resisting a society that severs body from mind, sexuality from commitment. Our bottom line must be a challenge to the strange credo of our sexual culture—that even bad copulation is better than good friendship.

Those in a Dry and Wonderless Marriage

If we feel trapped by a relationship that began with high ideals and eager vows of commitment, but that now seems arid and life-denying, is there any hope left?

The reason this type of situation seems hopeless is due to another cultural myth. Western thinking has assumed for centuries that what we think and feel shapes what we do. Applied to love, this means that if we have warm and gooey feelings toward the loved one, if we fall in love with them, then we will act on those feelings by carrying out loving actions: sending cards and flowers, buying gifts, holding somebody close, kissing, sharing a candlelit meal together.

It is, however, equally true (although our romance-infatuated culture has kept this a big secret) that what we do shapes what we feel. The point is well made by sociologist Tony Campolo, who writes that whenever he counsels individuals who claim the romance has gone from their marriage, and the only course open to them now is to end it, he tells them to do the following:

1. Each day make a new list of ten things that you would do for your spouse if you were in love.

2. Then each day, do the ten things that are on that list.[5]

Campolo's advice for putting the wonder back into intimacy sounds simple enough to be naive. But, as many couples have found, it actually works. And the reason it works is because of one vital truth: love is not just a feeling. It is actions. Love is not a force that overcomes us as we sit passively; it is an act of the will, something we choose to do. Even our fantasy life is an act of the will: fantasy can either draw us outside the committed relationship or help restore the wonder to it. Relationships, like houseplants, die of neglect.

Dave was thirty-seven and had been married for eight years to Jan when he began to notice Sarah. Sarah, who worked in the same office, was ten years younger than Jan and single. Was it his imagination, or was she making excuses to walk over to his side of the office whenever she could? He liked the way she laughed, the way her eyes twinkled. When they talked she seemed to understand him in a way Jan rarely did. She made him feel alive in a way he had not felt since the early days of his marriage. Come to think of it, had he ever felt this way about Jan? He was not sure if he had ever really been "in love" with Jan in this fizzy, heart-stopping way. What had he been missing out on all these years?

Dave had a choice. He could pursue his infatuation with Sarah. He could conclude that he and Jan had grown apart over the years and that he had a right to the kind of romantic excitement he had so far been denied. In short, he could have an affair. This in turn might lead to a divorce from Jan and a magical new life with Sarah.

Or he could laugh at himself, pull himself together and resolve to channel all his desire for romance, love, that new tingle-factor he was experiencing, into his marriage. He could work at falling in love with Jan for the first time. He could woo her as if she were the most stunning girl he had ever met. And he could keep Sarah as a friend, knowing that sex with her was simply out of the question. He could invite her and other colleagues home to meet Jan.

But nobody had ever told Dave that the second option was an option at all. It remains a secret many people in our culture have never heard. And Dave is a romantic, led by the heart. He had long dreamed of the kind of passionate romance he had seen in the old film Brief Encounter. It was natural that he should choose the first option, an affair with Sarah. As a result of the affair, he and Jan separated, although Jan was very reluctant to do so.

Shortly afterward the bright and bubbly Sarah found a younger man. As I write this, Dave's divorce is about to go through, and he now lives alone in a small apartment, regularly trawling nightclubs in search of that perfect partner who will make his heart fizz once again.

••

Like my journalist friend, many long to be revirginized into wonder.

••

Instead of keeping both a marriage to Jan and a friendship with Sarah, Dave lost both. Our culture is full of "Daves" of both sexes, their heads full of *Brief Encounter* myths: somewhere out there is the perfect partner, the one who will sweep me off my feet with a hitherto unknown passion; I must follow this passion wherever it might lead; once the passion has gone from a marriage it remains forever bland and beyond salvage; it is impossible to fall in love with the person you are married to.

These myths are as dangerous as they are all-pervasive. The reality is that romantic and sexual love works best only in the place it was designed to be enjoyed: a lifelong commitment to one other person. A cold, wonderless marriage can be rekindled into a blaze of thrill and sexual excitement. It happens time after time. It is exciting but usually kept secret in our society. Houseplants revive when watered and fed. A marriage is revived when partners refuse to allow it to die of neglect and are determined to work at it.

The implications of this for jaded Xers are remarkable. Wonder in relationships is not something that might or might not drift our way, like a rain cloud. It is not a hit-or-miss affair. Wonder can be rekindled. But it takes time and effort.[6]

Those Whose Pasts Have Deadened Intimacy

What hope is there for the man who meets the most wonderful woman he could have possibly imagined and longs to give himself to her fully for life, but knows he has slept with so many others that intimacy with her will be neither new nor special?

Fortunately we are not left alone in despair. The same gospel that offers us an ideal of wonder in relationship also holds out the promise of forgiveness when we smother that wonder through ignorance, stupidity or rebellion. Ronald Rolheiser, in his book of meditations *Forgotten Among the Lilies,* calls this healing of past mistakes "revirginization," the miraculous gift of wonder renewed. It is an experience of new birth.

The middle-aged journalist sitting opposite me had a twinkle in his eyes. "You could say I was a bit of a naughty boy in my youth." He winked and gave me knowing looks. "I did play the field a lot. In a way it was what people expected of you where I come from. The trouble was, when I met Jenny I felt sick at all that stuff I'd been doing for all those years. I was convinced that I'd ruined any chance of our sex life being special, because I'd done it all before with so many people.

"Anyway, I handed it over to God. I prayed that he would take away the past and let me start all over again. And you know, he did. I still regret all that sleeping around and all the people I must have hurt. That will never go away. But on our wedding night I was like a fifteen-year-old on his first date. I was really embarrassed, excited, fumbling and hesitant. It was as if I'd never been with any girl before." Like my journalist friend, many long to be revirginized into wonder.

It is not only those with a history of promiscuity who experience the death of wonder in intimacy. Jill had a history of short, intense flings; I met her when she was on her fourth marriage. Each of these relationships had fallen apart, according to Jill, due to "incompatibility." It soon became clear, however, that Jill's real problem was that she was a romance addict. She was using her serial monogamy as an attempt to realize the technicolor romances of her daydreams. But with each subsequent relationship the analogies with her bodice-ripping, candlelit, desert-island fantasies seemed to grow ever fainter.

Hope for Jill could never come from the dominant values of our therapeutic culture. She had followed the wide path of immediate personal gratification only to find that around several bends the path petered out, leading her in a bleak and rocky terrain, more alone than when she started the journey. Jill found, although she still finds it hard to admit this to herself, that her culture lied to her. It told her the big questions of meaning, truth, purpose and goodness were unanswerable and therefore unimportant; that all she could hope for was personal comfort and the thrill of the moment. She believed and pursued this passionately, only to end up having even this elude her.

There is hope for Jill, but it will come only from a brutal reassessment of the myths of her culture, myths that told her to forget questions of plot and purpose, to deny even that she was part of a bigger plot at all, and to focus on the details of life. Experience taught her the hard way that such details find their meaning only in a bigger context, that there must be more to life than self-gratification and living for the present. Jill must face up to the brokenness within her own life, trace the roots of her compulsions and challenge the unattainable fantasies that have motivated her whole adult life.[7]

Hope for Jill can come only through identifying the lie on which her life has been built and the unseen forces that have fed her compulsions. It will come when she can honestly admit her complicity with a culture of lies and be healed within. Jill too can be revirginized, but only through rebirth.

Indignation

Many Xers will read this chapter with the indignation their culture reserves for anyone who challenges its most fundamental assumptions. Even now many readers are probably asking, "What right do you have to tell us how to run our sex lives? If we're happy with what we're doing, then why can't we get on with it?" The answer, of course, is that I have no right at all to tell people how to express their sexuality. But the simple fact is that so many Xers are not happy with what they are doing.

A whole generation of young adults is doing what it likes, but they no longer like it very much. Xers have discovered the emptiness of casual sex, the boredom of commitment-free intimacy, the agonizing loneliness of a life lived without the openness and vulnerability of true friendship. They are longing for a fresh vision.

Mother Earth & the Wonder of Creation

••

At the outset the universe appears packed with will, intelligence, life and positive qualities; every tree is a nymph and every planet a god. Man himself is akin to the gods. The advance of knowledge gradually empties this rich and genial universe: first of its gods, then of its colours, smells, sounds and tastes, finally of solidity itself.
C. S. Lewis, preface to *The Hierarchy of Heaven and Earth* by D. E. Harding

I love old maps of the world, with their fat-cheeked babies blowing many-masted galleons, sea monsters dancing in the foam, Latin words and obscure planetary diagrams. I love the way the familiar outlines of countries look squashed and misshapen, as if they were left on a bus and sat on by a fat man. I try to imagine what it must have felt like, hundreds of years ago, to know that massive tracts of the globe were as yet unexplored and to imagine what lost cities, vast jungles and serpentine rivers might lie there.

I admit this is a terribly Eurocentric view and politically incorrect in the extreme. Most "undiscovered" lands were home to native inhabitants, and "discovery" in many cases meant bringing along the worst aspects of Western culture. But the romance of those old maps still lingers, with their promises of new horizons to be explored, new wonders to be found. It is an excitement that emerges in the best contemporary travel writing and sometimes in fantasy fiction. But somehow we seem incapable of recapturing the wonder of those old cartographers as they mapped the earth in all its mysterious glory.

I wonder how one of those mapmakers, or an explorer such as Vasco da Gama or Sebastian Cabot, would have reacted to Alan. It was 1994, just after the suicide of Kurt Cobain, singer of the grunge rock band Nirvana and heralded by some as the voice of his generation. We were discussing why young adults were killing

> According to this view, human beings are merely a complex form of machine that has evolved. Even human personality and emotions such as love are part of the machine. In the dry worldview of naturalism the earth is an impersonal commodity to be used and exploited.

themselves in such large and growing numbers. I asked Alan, who was nineteen, why he believed there had been such a rash of sympathetic suicides by Cobain's contemporaries across North America and Europe.

He thought for a while. "It has a lot to do with depression, turning in on yourself. But there's also a sense that there's nothing much worth living for. You've experienced everything life has to offer. You've been to lots of places, met lots of people, and you're still feeling bored and miserable. You know nothing's ever going to change, so what's there to stick around for?"

For Alan and many others like him, suicide has become just another lifestyle option, a last high, a one-way ticket to the only territory still unexplored. For many Xers the real, material world around them is prosaic and ordinary, the banal backdrop to a bored existence.

Such opinions are no longer minor streams in the current thinking of young adults. They have become a powerful torrent. But what are the tributaries that have contributed to the flow?

The Rise of Scientific Materialism

One reason for the stripping away of wonder from the earth has been the direction of Western science and technology over the past three hundred years. Beginning in the late seventeenth century, under the influence of thinkers such as Descartes and Newton, people increasingly started to describe the natural world as a machine that ran according to the laws of cause and effect. At first this was held in tension with a belief in God—sometimes the God of the Bible, sometimes a more distant, shadowy "First Principle." If the earth was a complex mechanism, God was the watchmaker.

It was not long until the rise of naturalism, the view that the physical universe is all there is. According to this view, human beings are merely a complex form of machine that has evolved. Even human personality and emotions such as love are part of the machine. In the dry worldview of naturalism the earth is an impersonal commodity to be used and exploited.

Those things that provoke wonder in the human psyche—the appreciation of beauty, an encounter of surprise and awe, respect for otherness, the dimension of the spirit—are excluded. Scientific materialism is reductionist—it reduces the rich variety of life to a single track—and among those things that are reduced are the roots of wonder.

The Communications Revolution

Another tributary into the current of indifference has been the dramatic boom in communications technology combined with our ever more sophisticated means of transportation. It is easy to forget just how recently this has come about. Awhile ago I spoke to an elderly woman born before Wilbur and Orville Wright designed and flew the first powered airplane in 1903, and well before 1926, when John Logie Baird first transmitted moving images. By the end of the same century we have satellite and cable TV, mobile phones, fax, the Internet, e-mail, FM radio, pagers and a global network of international airports.

Nowhere is really remote and undiscovered anymore. We watch in intimate detail the lives of rain forest tribes, foreign royalty and those who live in the snows of northern Canada. Television news brings instant images from every part of the globe. I might never have spoken to my next-door neighbor, but I can watch a man in Kiev eating breakfast and chat to somebody in their bathtub in Toowoomba.

Such massive, global communications are an astounding achievement. But the effect has been a little like casual sex. Promiscuous media consumption has a deadening effect on our capacity for awe before

> Space, however, was not the final frontier it promised to be. To be sure, it gripped imaginations for much of the second half of the twentieth century. But now space is beginning to look more like a junkyard.

the strange and exotic. For us, nothing is new anymore. We have been everywhere, seen everybody, done everything.

Virtual Existence

It is not simply that communications saturation has left us indifferent to things that would have astonished a previous age. In an age of electronic communications, events in the physical world become less and less important to our perception of what is "real" and what matters.

Media critic Marshall McLuhan said we live in a global village. If that is true, then the media are the village gossips, endlessly chattering about trivia, setting the agenda for the rest of us. They are voices that no one in the village can escape.

Like all good gossips, the media not only recount stories but also invent them. We discuss at length the plots of last night's soaps and sitcoms. To tell what happened in the real world—maybe we were slumped on a couch, occasionally shouting at the kids—is too indescribably boring to mention. The "reality" of last night becomes a media-created virtual reality.

Eighteenth-century Irish philosopher George Berkeley once asked whether a tree that fell unseen by human eye can in any real sense be said to have fallen at all. In today's culture many events, particularly in the realm of politics, are not considered real unless the media are watching.

Journalist Simon Hoggart says we are living in "the era of the permanent campaign,"[1] where political decisions are made less for their effectiveness or morality than for their capacity to boost somebody's chances of reelection. Image triumphs over substance and sound bite over policy. Embodied, everyday existence ceases to be much of an end in itself. It becomes simply the raw material to be reported or filmed.

Thanks to TV even our warfare has become entertainment. During the Gulf War the bloody reality of death was sanitized into an arcade game by the computerized images of precision bombing: Zap! Pow! Gotcha!

Into Cyberspace

When we grew bored with the earth, we restored our sense of wonder by looking into space. Captain Kirk, Neil Armstrong, Dr. Who, Carl Sagan, Darth Vader and a host of sci-fi novelists offered to help us boldly go where no one had gone before.

Space, however, was not the final frontier it promised to be. To be sure, it gripped imaginations for much of the second half of the twentieth century. But now space is beginning to look more like a junkyard. By 1996 the U.S. Space Surveillance Center was saying there were some 8,847 objects whizzing around the earth, not to mention smaller items such as nuts and bolts from spacecraft. One estimate puts the number of fragments of human debris in orbit at 35 million. Today outer space has been replaced by the weird and wonderful world of cyberspace as the haunt of avant-garde novelists and teen fantasy.

The term *cyberspace* was coined in the 1980s by the novelist William Gibson to describe the extrageographical, virtual "universe" inside the worldwide computer network, the Internet. In this sense cyberspace does not exist in space and time at all. It is not a location but a vast complex of computer links crisscrossing the globe. It is a computer-generated place without any tangible reality, and yet "real" events happen there that have a real effect in daily life. We shop there, play there, socialize there, even divorce and worship there.

To an older generation the idea of discovering a parallel universe inside one's typewriter would have seemed bizarre. C. S. Lewis and Lewis Carroll found new worlds inside wardrobes and mirrors, but Narnia and Wonderland were the stuff of children's fantasy. To us the Internet is becoming a real home, every bit as much as the four walls that surround us. If baby boomers are couch potatoes, busters are "mouse" potatoes, clicking their way ever deeper into the vast, unexplored wonderland of cyberspace.

As more and more events "happen" in virtual reality, our physical bodies become less and less important to us. The outside world grows less glamorous compared with the hallucinatory, unbounded universe inside our computers. The heroes and explorers of today's fiction are less likely to be the physically strong superhero than the techno-nerd, the isolated computer hacker who dares to enter the unknown territories inside his PC and emerge triumphant.

As the electronic, virtual world of the Internet bids to replace the physical world of books, paper and solid objects, the effect diminishes our embodiment. Everyday physical life becomes the pale antechamber to which we return for refueling, the gray terminal where we rest between our flights of fantasy.

Virtually Religious

We might think religion would help reenchant the earth. Ironically, the ways religious experience have tended to be defined (both by outside observers and by many believers) have had the effect of further diminishing the sacredness of everyday life.

In 1912 French sociologist Émile Durkheim published *Elementary Forms of the Religious Life*. In it he claimed all religions have one thing in common: they all classify reality into two distinct categories, profane and sacred.

The profane is what is familiar, routine and boring—the eating, sleeping and working that forms the backdrop to existence. The sacred, on the other hand, is an ideal dimension, set apart from the ordinary. The sacred, according to Durkheim, is a transcendent, ideal realm, above the everyday. It is the realm of awe, mystery, excitement, to be accessed in special places and through special rites.

The home is profane; the church or temple is sacred. An electrician or banana picker is profane; a clergyman or shaman is sacred. The profane pushes us deeper into our earthly life, while the sacred pulls us above it into a realm of pure spirit.

Durkheim's classifications exerted a significant influence on the study of religion. They have been the spectacles through which most analysts have viewed and categorized all religious experience. In their search for the special places, people and realms where the sacred may be found, such writers use categories that not only are alien to biblical Christianity but also reinforce the banality of the real world. As they look at life through these bifocal lenses of dualism, everything that has not been in some way sanctified is written off as secular or ordinary. We are denied a sense of wonder in the everyday.

If this is at odds with a biblical worldview, how have churches fared in offering a radically alternative vision? Sadly, Christians have all too often conspired with the bifocal vision of academics. Many believers carve life up into categories of sacred and secular, elevating the spiritual and despising the material, viewing human nature as a nonmaterial soul or spirit trapped in base matter but longing to soar to disembodied, heavenly realms.

Such a picture bears little relation to the biblical view of human nature or life after death. It has more in common with the second-century heresy of Gnosticism, which saw matter as irredeemably evil, a prison for pure spirit, which could escape only through esoteric knowledge and rituals.

To be an Xer is to inherit a drab, functional world of mundane and familiar objects, a world drained of wonder. But we have learned well the lessons taught by our culture, that excitement and awe are not found in the mundane. They are found only in escapism. Gnosticism has returned. We are a generation desperately looking for ways to reenchant the earth, to see the magical in the mundane and the glory in the everyday. We recognize that something vital has been lost.

Looking for Enchantment in All the Wrong Places

This state of affairs, as we discussed earlier in our story of G. K. Chesterton, is an exact parallel to the late nineteenth century. Science, it was thought, held all the answers. All humanity's problems could be solved through rational, humanistic endeavor. Religion was a fossil from a past age of ignorance and superstition.

Yet even as the death of God was being proclaimed by the intellectuals, a host of other gods began to move in. Interest in the occult blossomed, and séances—meetings where spiritualists tried to receive messages from the dead—became commonplace in middle-class drawing rooms.

•••

We are a generation desperately looking for ways to reenchant the earth, to see the magical in the mundane and the glory in the everyday. We recognize that something vital has been lost.

•••

A group of New York occultists led by the Russian-born Madame Blavatsky (Elena Petrovna) founded the Theosophical Society in 1875, a combination of spiritualism, Eastern mystical religion and the occult. In 1887 the Hermetic Order of the Golden Dawn was set up in London. Its founders claimed their esoteric teachings came from a group of powerful magicians who were secretly working for the benefit of the world. Their goal was "higher magic," or union with the divine, attained through clairvoyance, astral projection and other magical practices. The Dawn became a crucial step in the development of Western occultism.

One of the early members of the Golden Dawn was Aleister Crowley (born in 1875 to a Plymouth Brethren family), who was to become the most significant magician of the modern era and a major influence on contemporary Satanists. Crowley adopted for himself the title "The Great Beast," a description of the antichrist in the book of Revelation. After a quarrel with the leadership of the Golden Dawn he traveled the world in search of occult knowledge, eventually founding what he called his new religion, based on the principle "Do what thou wilt shall be the whole of the Law." His followers became notorious for their strange ceremonies, unrestrained sexuality and drug use.

At the same time more mainline esoteric groups such as the Freemasons and a range of exotic Eastern religions found a new lease on life in the West, even among the apparently dry, rational leaders of Victorian society. The creator of Sherlock Holmes, Arthur Conan Doyle, devoted the latter part of his life to occultism and his attempts to photograph fairies. Sir James Frazer's book The Golden Bough (1890) became required reading for the educated classes, with its study of traditional and esoteric religions from around the globe, and influenced the religious thinking of a generation. The Ouija board became commonplace in upper-class salons.

This intriguing period of British and American life points to one overwhelming conclusion: people cannot live in a disenchanted universe. Drain away orthodox religion and our hunger for wonder and mystery will let the old gods return.

Generation X, raised in an age of unprecedented scientific advance and materialistic optimism, has been taught to build a universe on technology, progress and pragmatism. Our gurus were supposed to be economists, advertisers and chiefs of industry, but like our Victorian forebears, we looked to a different set of gurus to reenchant the world. Seeing in churches only a dry formalism, but still yearning to inhabit a sacred earth, many have embarked on a spiritual journey similar to that of the late Victorians.

> **Most neopagans are suspicious of any creed, which they see as an attempt by the powerful to impose a dogma on somebody else.**

For many Xers the quest for the sacred remains at the level of buying Arthurian novels, CDs of Gregorian chants and posters of Celtic art. But for many others the quest for mystery and meaning is more serious. If the path of reenchantment for the late Victorians wound through Ouija boards, spiritualism and the East, the path chosen by many today is more likely to pass through the ancient traditions of their native lands.

Neopagans and Earth Goddesses

Pagan stems from the Latin *paganus,* meaning "one from the countryside" (*pagus,* "a village"). The neopagans of today trace their ancestry back to the old nature religions of pre-Christian Europe and North America. The movement includes witchcraft (also known as Wicca or "the craft"), Native American spirituality, and an eclectic mix of gods and mythologies from the classical Mediterranean and the Norse and Celtic lands of northern Europe. Most adherents exclude from their frame of reference monotheistic faiths such as Christianity, Judaism and Islam, as well as Eastern religions and Satanism. The common core to an otherwise diverse movement is a reverence for the natural world.

It is difficult to assess the scale of the current neopagan revival in the West. In 1989 the Occult Census of Great Britain estimated around 250,000 British could be classed as pagans or witches, with hundreds of thousands more pursuing an interest in astrology, alternative healing and psychic powers. Anthropologist David Burnett suggests a figure closer to 100,000 practicing pagans, the majority being young adults.[2] In nominally Roman Catholic France it is estimated that there are five times as many practicing witches as Catholic priests.

No precise figures exist for North America, but every major population center has a growing community that identifies with the ideals of neopaganism. Whatever the exact numbers, it is clear that large numbers of young adults in the West are digging into their own native spiritual traditions in search of wonder and a basis for reverence toward the earth.

Neopaganism is no single body of beliefs but encourages a broad diversity of attitudes and practices. Most neopagans are suspicious of any creed, which they see as an attempt by the powerful to impose a dogma on somebody else. There are, however, certain focuses of unity. One path shared by most neopagans is belief in an earth goddess.

In the ancient cultures of Greece, Rome, Northern Europe and among Native Americans, the concept of the earth as mother was more than just a figure of speech. Earth itself was personified as a female divinity (to the Iroquois, Eithinoha; to the Greeks, Gaia; to the Canaanites, Ashtoreth), worshiped as the sustainer of all life on earth. She was not viewed as a creator separate from the creation, as Christians view God. Rather she was often seen as a pantheistic goddess, immanent in nature.

Advocates of the goddess cult today claim support from the British atmospheric scientist James Lovelock's "Gaia hypothesis," published in 1979. This suggests that the astonishingly fine balance of chemical and physical conditions on the earth's surface, in its atmosphere and oceans, points to the earth's being a single, self-regulating organism, in effect a living being. Lovelock himself claims to be an agnostic in matters of religion, but others have taken his ideas as support for a reality behind the old myths of Mother Earth—an immortal, immanent life force running through all creation.

So according to the neopagan, if the earth itself is divine, then reverence for the earth becomes a sacred duty, and sensitivity to the natural world a religious obligation.

Craving Wonder

To many older people the rediscovery of paganism and goddess worship among young Westerners seems baffling and incomprehensible. To most Xers, however, the very bafflement of others itself seems odd. We rightly recognize the anguish of living in a universe stripped of wonder, a universe from which all purpose, all presence, all the magic has been drained. The impulse behind such searching is a natural, healthy rebellion against the reductionisms of twentieth-century secular humanism, which so many of us were brought up to take as axiomatic.

Yet I and many others find a fulfillment of our rebellion, our yearnings, not in neopaganism, witchcraft or the occult but in historic Christianity. Why did goddess worshipers in Greece and Rome turn to embrace the loving heavenly Father offered by the early Christian martyrs? How did the fresh vision of Christianity inspire the greatest Celtic artists to leave paganism and produce masterpieces such as the Book of Kells, the Lindisfarne Gospels and the intricate tracery of Celtic crosses?

Poems, Heroes and Monsters

When I was in primary school, about seven or eight years old, I sometimes failed to show up for classes. Eventually one teacher took the time to find out where I was when I should have been in class. She found me curled up with tales about the gods, goddesses and heroes of the ancient Mediterranean. Years later I still find my imagination runs riot at the mention of the names that gripped my childhood imagination: Orpheus, Zeus, Cerberus, Ariadne, Ulysses, the Cyclops.

Their world was one of adventure, heroism, tragedy, beasts, battles, passion and wonder. It was a world of poetry and fantasy. But ask that young boy whether the tales were true, and I suspect I would have said something like: "No, of course not. They're just stories. They're not real!"

I strongly suspect that if you had asked an ancient Greek or Roman the same question, the response would not have been so different. The gods inhabited a poetic world, a world whispered into existence around fires on dark evenings. Their home was a wonderland like that dreamed up by Alice as she dozed on the banks of an Oxfordshire river. Their reality was a poetic reality, their "truth" a poetic truth.[3]

Sometimes my small son peers down from his bunk bed and refuses to cross the darkened room in case the monsters get him. It is a fear beyond reason. Any self-respecting monster that happened to be in the room would not hesitate to slither over to his bed and scoop him out. But mythology has its secrets that reason will never grasp. The bed is a place of safety, the floor an alien territory guarded by shadow creatures. My son's monsters say more about his hungry imagination than about their hungry stomachs.

••

Here is the astounding innovation. In Christianity the poetic wonder of paganism leaves the twilight world of the hearth and enters the full sunlit glare of history. Now the magic not only lies in our imagination but treads the streets of first-century Palestine.

••

The more astute among today's neopagan writers readily admit much the same about their spirituality. Their return to the figures of classical mythology is a way of talking not so much about the world "out there" as about the world "in here," in their own heads. Images such as the goddess are helpful archetypes, myths that project onto the screen of nature the structures of our own imagination. They are tales that embody the ideals we value and seek to live by: femininity, love, mystery, bravery.

This makes for wonderful storytelling but bad religion. The bottom line becomes not whether beliefs are coherent and reasonable but whether they meet a felt need in the heart of the individual. It is up to us to find a mythology that "fits," regardless of its historical or factual basis. In reaction to the dry rationalism of the scientific West, pagans are pushing to the other extreme.

By contrast, biblical Christianity is firmly rooted in history, in the public world of observable facts. The events of the New Testament were seen by countless eyewitnesses. The books of the New

Testament, the foundational documents of the faith, have been subject to more scrutiny by historians down the ages than any other ancient works. We possess more manuscripts attesting to the antiquity and authenticity of the New Testament books than any other work from the ancient world.

Christian tradition has concurred with the apostle Paul's insistence that the key events on which Christianity rests, such as Christ's resurrection from death, are rooted firmly in historical events. He writes to the believers in the city of Corinth, a city steeped in the myths of classical paganism: "If there is no resurrection of the dead, then not even Christ has been raised. And if Christ has not been raised, our preaching is useless and so is your faith. More than that, we are then found to be false witnesses about God, for we have testified about God that he raised Christ from the dead."[4]

Here is the astounding innovation. In Christianity the poetic wonder of paganism leaves the twilight world of the hearth and enters the full sunlit glare of history. Now the magic not only lies in our imagination but treads the streets of first-century Palestine.

As a child I walked the golden paths of Mount Olympus in my imagination. As an adult I recently walked the dry earth paths of the Mount of Olives. In the coming of Christ something happened that paganism had only dreamed about and told as wild stories. Now the real earth was enchanted, the real skies filled with angelic beings, and in a real garden a real God battled against the real powers of Hades.

The small boy grew up to discover that the fulfillment of paganism was not to be found in paganism. The gods, goddesses and heroes pointed beyond themselves to something bigger and more marvelous. Like the people of the ancient world, the boy awoke from the daydreams of wonderland only to find that the world about him was a real theater of glory.

Sanitized Goddesses

Advocates of the neopagan revival claim it offers a basis for the durable values of community, trust and goodness so desperately sought by a numbed generation. But it is easy for those in search of ancient wisdom to have a sentimental view of ancient paganism. Many today, particularly members of the Green movement and some radical feminists, view paganism through soft-focus, rose-colored glasses. They claim we need to return to a hypothetical age of antiquity when worship of the goddess ensured that the qualities of the feminine held sway in society and engendered a reverence for the earth.

This vision, however, fundamentally distorts what we know of goddesses in the ancient world. Most of them were far from the universal, benevolent mothers projected by today's neopagans. Many of the goddesses of the ancient Near East—Aphrodite in Corinth, Mylitta in Babylon and Cybele in Syria—demanded temple prostitution.

Other ancient goddesses were embodiments of pure evil. The Hindu mother-deity Kali is pictured carrying a sword, a noose and a cup made from half a human skull and filled with blood; her earrings are dead human babies and her belt is decorated with freshly severed human hands! The Ugaritic goddess Ishtar is seen in legend as a bloodthirsty psychopath. Tanit of Carthage was consort to the god Baal, and both demanded the sacrifice of hundreds of live human babies.

The goddesses and gods of ancient Greece and Rome made up a severely dysfunctional family, one which makes the worst families of today look like havens of tranquillity. Zeus and Apollo repeatedly raped and then imprisoned or killed female mortals. Artemis, patron deity of Ephesus, was associated with ritualized death, and human sacrifice was sometimes practiced by her followers.

There is no mystery why the ancient world turned its back on paganism. By the third century A.D. *pagan* had become a term of abuse in the Roman Empire. Even ancient storytellers started censuring the behavior of their deities, the nightmare soap-opera families of antiquity. The Roman poet Ovid even refers to the gods' "celestial crimes."

In practice the ancients tended to find their worldview in the secular values of their state: allegiance to the emperor, obedience to the laws of their land. "Religious" observance involved private devotion but was largely irrelevant to public life, except insofar as attendance at its rituals—such as sacrifice—helped ensure social conformity. The pagan gods were simply not big enough, good enough, powerful or real enough to be a basis for truth, dignity and morals. Trusting these gods would be like us turning to comic books for a guide to spirituality and ethics today.

But those on neopagan paths ignore the historical reality of paganism, preferring a sanitized version custom-made for environmentally aware, spiritually starved postmoderns. Sentimentalized representations of pagan life gloss over harsh truths of history. For every benevolent Gaia there was a bloody Artemis or Ishtar. The Iroquois, who worshiped the earth goddess Eithinoha—Our Mother—also massacred their neighbors the Huron.

Sanitizing Selfishness or Erasing the Self
Christians believe we inhabit a moral universe where our concepts of good and evil exist because they are rooted in the character of the Creator himself. For the Christian the ultimate value is self-sacrificing love, following the example of Christ. The God who cares for widows, orphans and outsiders and the Christ who gives himself for others are our role models. True power for the Christian can be only relational and sacrificial.

On the other hand, the witch Starhawk, one of the leaders of the

Wiccan revival and a bestselling author, writes that the goal of Wicca is about "personal power. We all strive to increase our power-from-within."[5] The way to increase this inner power is through magic. All gods, myths, landscapes, rituals and relationships are means to inner, personal empowerment. There is little basis for compassion built into pagan philosophy. It begins to look more like sanctified selfishness.

Pagans might reply that this is a misunderstanding of their faith, that paganism is essentially relational, since in a pantheistic system we are all inseparably bound together. Books about the goddess are filled with claims that since she is the life force of the whole earth, we all participate in that life. Pagans criticize the Christian God, whom they wrongly stereotype as masculine, remote, warlike and indifferent, as offering little basis for an ethic of global harmony.

In fact, for all its noble ideals, the pantheism of neopaganism actually undermines personal dignity. If earth, sky, sea, animals, plants and humans are merely dimensions of a universal goddess, all that ultimately matters is the grand whole. No part of that whole can claim to have more significance than any other. We have a role only insofar as we use ritual to immerse ourselves in the broad flow of life. None of us is of fundamental importance or value in ourselves. We function only as blurred parts of a bigger pattern, a pattern that is beyond our imposed categories of right and wrong.

> All gods, myths, landscapes, rituals and relationships are means to inner, personal empowerment. There is little basis for compassion built into pagan philosophy. It begins to look more like sanctified selfishness.

Contemporary witches are correct to say that Wicca does not have a concept of good and evil.[6] Sin becomes a meaningless concept if the ultimate reality is the goddess, who embodies in herself all light and dark, right and wrong, truth and falsehood. The pagan answer to our quest for personal values is that we have no personal value. Its advice to a generation longing to erase selfishness is to erase the self. If this seems depressing, there are other alternatives to consider in the next chapter.

7

Thanking Someone for the Earth

••

Earth's crammed with heaven,
And every common bush afire with God:
But only he who sees, takes off his shoes.
Elizabeth Barrett Browning, *Aurora Leigh*

*W*e are a generation in search of older gods, gods who will repair the damage done to the earth in the name of our cultural idols of individualism, materialism and technology. The Christian claim is that these dreams and aspirations are met in the God of the Bible, a God who entered history in the person of Jesus of Nazareth.

Christianity asserts that creation is a gift, a visible reminder of the Creator, and that humans are called to be God's caring stewards of the earth. It has been said that the crisis of atheists is when they feel overwhelmed by the sheer gift of life but have nobody to thank.

Wonder Rediscovered

This sense of gratitude before the gifts of God in creation is fundamental to many of the psalms in the Bible. The writers of the psalms have an affinity with the beauty of creation just as much as any pagan or nature-mystic. But they depart from paganism when they recognize it all as the handiwork of a loving, personal Creator. In Psalm 148 the imagery of nature tumbles over itself in grateful torrents.

Praise the LORD from the earth,
you great sea creatures and all ocean depths,
lightning and hail, snow and clouds,
stormy winds that do his bidding,
you mountains and all hills,
fruit trees and all cedars,
wild animals and all cattle,
small creatures and flying birds,
kings of the earth and all nations,
you princes and all rulers on earth,
young men and maidens,
old men and children.[1]

....

Like royalty, God is robed in splendor, but God's robe is his creation, the natural world. Creation is charged up with his glory, the visible majesty radiating from him.

....

The poet moves beyond paganism in his gratitude that the gift has a personal giver:

Let them praise the name of the LORD,
for he commanded and they were created.
He set them in place for ever and ever;
he gave a decree that will never pass away.[2]

God's Clothing
In the perspective of historic Christianity, however, the earth is not just a gift from God. It actually offers a glimpse into the life of God

himself. The psalms make explicit something implied throughout Scripture: the creation is an extension of the Creator, his "clothing."

O LORD my God, you are very great;
　　you are clothed with splendor and majesty.
He wraps himself in light as with a garment.[3]
He made darkness his covering, his canopy around him—
　　the dark rain clouds of the sky.[4]

God himself might be invisible to the human eye, but the "splendor and majesty" that clothe him are the evidence of his presence. Like royalty, God is robed in splendor, but God's robe is his creation, the natural world.

God is present in the skies, wind, fire and storms. Creation is charged up with his glory, the visible majesty radiating from him. The Hebrews called it the *shekinah,* the glory that shines from God as the evidence of his presence on earth. The seraphs who address Isaiah remind him that the *shekinah* of the Creator is not a remote, distant force but fills the globe. Every twig and branch, cloud and star point beyond themselves to a personal presence:

Holy, holy, holy is the LORD Almighty;
　　the whole earth is full of his glory.[5]

There is another way, however, in which the Christian understanding of nature differs from that of the secular humanists and the neopagans, an issue of vital concern to Generation X. It is the question of how we react to the evil and brokenness in our world.

Both secularists and pagans assume, in their different ways, that the world cannot be fundamentally different from the way it is at present. Secularists see only a closed system of cause and effect and natural laws; pagans see people simply as part of the cosmic life force, able to experience their interconnectedness but unable to stand aside and question it. Paganism accounts for the evident evil in the system with tales of mischievous gods and goddesses, or else by claiming that a universal god or goddess embodies not only good but also evil. Neither option gives a reassuring basis for human moral action or for believing that evil has an antidote.

Christianity, however, insists that the present state of our world is not the way it was meant to be. Evil is a reality, both in the natural world and in the human heart. For Christians there is space to collaborate with the redemptive purposes of God, in whom there is no darkness at all, in bringing healing to creation.

Stewards of the Earth

As we interact with the created world we not only encounter the wonder of the earth but also find the roots of our own identity. In the Bible's opening story in the book of Genesis, God makes human beings so they can be in relationship with him, with each other and with the earth.

The poet of Genesis has described the origins of the earth, the skies, the oceans, plant life and animal life, and now his tumbling torrent of Hebraic verse reaches a crescendo:

Then God said, "Let us make man in our image, in our likeness, and let them rule over the fish of the sea and the birds of the air, over the livestock, over all the earth, and over all the creatures that move along the ground."

So God created man in his own image,
in the image of God he created him;
male and female he created them.[6]

We discover our full humanity as stewards of the earth, being its responsible caretakers. Ours is the task of trusted intermediaries, representing creation to God and God to creation.

We have a calling, individually and in community, to tend the earth and draw out its potential. Not just for our own sake, although this is important, but for God's sake as well. One dimension of this is ecological, the calling to protect and care for the earth by careful use of its resources. No good manager stands by twiddling her thumbs while the object of her care is being destroyed.

••

We discover our full humanity as stewards of the earth, being its responsible caretakers. Ours is the task of trusted intermediaries, representing creation to God and God to creation.

••

But there is more to our calling on earth than firefighting. In the verse immediately following the creation of humans we are told: "God blessed them and said to them, 'Be fruitful and increase in number; fill the earth and subdue it. Rule over the fish of the sea and the birds of the air and over every living creature that moves on the ground.' "[7] This verse is sometimes called the "cultural mandate" to humans. We are to take the raw materials of the earth and use them creatively. We are not simply to live close to nature (as many romantics and ecologists would have it) but to be creative and cultural.

God in effect tells his newly created images that he has left their earth unfinished. It is now up to them to draw out its latent potential in terms of agriculture, the arts, economics, architecture, science and so on. It is as we carry out our distinctive callings to be teachers, fashion designers, politicians, road sweepers, musicians, students, business executives and artists that we live as the image of God on earth. We are called to be creative stewards of creation.

An announcement of this commission is also given in Genesis: "The LORD God took the man [*Adam* means 'humanity'] and put him in the Garden of Eden to work it and take care of it."[8] In the Genesis account stewardship over the earth has two dimensions: working it and caring for it. Christians have a God-given mandate for ecology. The Hebrew word used for "caring," *samar,* means to watch, protect, tend and keep from harm. Christians should be in the forefront of environmental concern, because our motivation to tend the planet and keep it safe is a primary calling from God. This is no mandate for some back-to-nature, pastoral ideal. The other word used in the commission, *abad,* means to work the earth, to serve it, to use it creatively. It is a reminder that the human task is to take the raw material of creation and develop it creatively as described at the end of the first chapter of Genesis. The Bible tells us that it is our calling to find satisfaction and identity in all our culture-forming tasks—art, science and business as much as agriculture and botany.

Creation Renewed
The pagan vision is of the universal harmony of all nature on an innocent earth. It is a fine dream that has inspired cultures of great art and literature from the ancient world to the classical revivalists of Renaissance Europe and among modern-day pagan idealists.

But where does the dream come from? And how is it to be attained? In reality it is Christianity alone that claims our dreams of Eden are a nostalgia for a real place, a lost innocence. Christianity alone claims that the earth will one day be renewed, that a day will come when all the highest dreams of paganism become a reality. It is a vision elaborated in the book of Revelation (see especially chapter 21) and foreseen by the Hebrew prophets (for example, in Isaiah 60). It is a vision of a day when the lion and lamb will lie together, swords will be beaten into plowshares, and all nations, genders and races of the earth will live together in harmony.

For now Christians know that as stewards we are called to be the creative caretakers of a world that is flawed, but nonetheless still charged with the glory of its Creator. We are also to be those who

are "looking for the city that is to come,"[9] signposts to the final
fulfillment of the dreams of the ages, a day when the earth will be
filled with the innocent wonder of a fresh new morning and the old
order of things will have passed away.

God: The Wonder of Encounter

••

But then I must remind myself we are living creatures—we have
religious impulses—we must—and yet into what cracks do these
impulses flow in a world without religion? It is something I think
about every day. Sometimes I think it is the only thing I should be
thinking about.

Douglas Coupland, *Life After God*

*O*ne could almost feel sorry for secular humanists such as
Karl Marx, Bertrand Russell, Julian Huxley, A. J. Ayer and Richard
Dawkins. For so long things appeared to be going their way. But
just as final victory seemed certain and the last rumors of gods,
angels and demons appeared to have been killed off, back they all
came with renewed vigor. God is having the last laugh. Of all the
endangered species on the earth today, *Homo secularus* looks least
likely to survive.

Quite a reversal from the picture of religion in the modern world
that held sway from the nineteenth century to as recently as the
1970s! Victorian thinkers such as Herbert Spencer and Thomas
Huxley wrenched the theory of evolution from biology, applied it
to society and renamed it "progress." Just as animal species that
survive were considered fitter and better adapted to their conditions,
so too the newer forms of society—scientific, rational and indus-

trial—were thought to be superior. Religion was a feature of preindustrial, primitive cultures, the product of a worldview that was no longer tenable.

It is sobering to realize that for all its sound and fury, secularism was a brief aberration in history. Despite all the best efforts of atheists, the children they spawned are returning to religion in droves. Or perhaps their rebellion in turning toward God has been because of the very secularism of their parents. They have seen the products of "progress" and "enlightenment" and do not like what they see.

Religious faith is resurgent around the globe. Fundamentalist Islam grips the hearts of idealistic young men in numerous countries. Across the United States "megachurches" of over two thousand members flourish in many towns and cities. Fully 40 percent of all Americans are in church on any given Sunday.

> **The postmodern world is deeply suspicious of any claims to absolute truth, including the truths of secularism. All "isms" are suspect.**

A range of alternative religious options are busy crowding into the Western marketplace. Indigenous traditions such as paganism, Native American spirituality and shamanism are being rediscovered. New Age stores sell tarot cards, small pyramids, healing crystals and the I Ching. Angels too have made a striking comeback, with large sections of bookstores and even whole shops devoted to the sale of angel books, pictures, models, hangings and ornaments.

Relatively True

For most people in the West, however, the return to faith is no simple return to presecularism. For all the resurgence of interest in the spiritual, the official figures for church attendance continue to slide, particularly in Europe. The Church of England's 1996 report *Youth A Part* revealed that church attendance of fourteen- to twenty-one one-year-olds dropped by over a third in the seven years between 1987 and 1994. The U.S. too is seeing a gradual decline in overall church attendance, the slide of the mainline denominations (such as Methodists, Episcopalians and Presbyterians) being particularly steep.

Many thinkers are increasingly dividing the history of the West into three eras: the premodern (up to the eighteenth century), the modern (from the eighteenth century to somewhere around the late 1960s or early 1970s) and the postmodern (the present era). The main characteristic of the postmodern era is that all the big ideas—faiths, philosophies and "isms"—of the previous two eras have collapsed.

In religious terms, if premodernity was the era dominated by a single religion—Christianity—modernity was dominated by a single dogma—secular progress. What then of postmodernity? The postmodern world is motivated by a single impulse—personal choice.

If a medieval peasant had been asked what the bottom line of religion is, she might have said: "That God exists and can be known through the church." If a Victorian secularist had been asked the same question, he might have said: "The fact that God doesn't exist, because we have no scientific proof that he does."

But ask the same question of a Generation Xer, raised in a climate of postmodernity, and he or she is more likely to say: "It's up to everybody to find whatever is true for them." The postmodern world is deeply suspicious of any claims to absolute truth, including the truths of secularism. All "isms" are suspect: Marxism is discredited; many of the older, established churches are slowly emptying. No single vision commands such widespread support as relativism, the view that there are no absolutes binding on anybody.

It must be over a decade since anyone said to me, "You're a

Christian—give me some proof that God actually exists." On the other hand, scarcely a month goes by without someone in their teens or twenties asking why Christians feel the need to convince everybody else that their faith is true—or else telling me with dogmatic certainty that "all religions are the same"!

I remember one student staring at me in utter disbelief when I claimed that Christianity might be true in a way that other systems were not. She could hardly understand what I was saying: "So you're saying it's true for you. But if somebody else finds something different that is just as true for them, then how can you say your way is better? And anyway, all the religions are saying the same things, aren't they?"

There has been a change in the popular consciousness over the past two decades or so. We have moved from the assumption that if something is true a contradictory view must be untrue; that somewhere out there is a single "big picture" that is true for everybody and that religion and philosophy have to discover. It is now customary to believe that nobody has a monopoly on truth, that there is probably no single "big story" to be found. The best we can do is find something that works for us and makes us happy.

The way this is expressed in religious terms is that "ultimate reality" is an unknowable mystery that we each need to encounter in our own way. Author Matthew Fox is typical of the postmodern mindset when he likens the religious quest to the attempt to draw water from a deep underground river. The representatives of all religions and philosophies sit around their wells lowering buckets. Each might believe his or hers is the only true well, but all wells ultimately descend to the river that is God, who is beyond all definitions and all systems.

This model of religious "truth" has an enormous appeal for Xers, whose dominant value is relational. Xers believe they have found a key to greater global harmony and tolerance in this view that teaches all religions are equally valid, all truth relative, all that matters is whether it works for you. But where has this new relativist consensus come from?

Born to Shop

Most people throughout most of human history have lived at a subsistence level in societies where people worked to stay alive. Workers provided for the immediate needs of their own families and villages, food was grown locally, clothes were made by local people. The one exception to this was royalty and nobility, those with the wealth to have others farm, manufacture and produce luxury goods for them.

In the West from the late nineteenth century on this pattern changed dramatically. For the first time techniques of mass production and faster means of transportation meant more goods than were needed for personal survival could be produced. The kind of luxuries formerly restricted to the ruling classes started to become a possibility for people at all levels of society. Brand names, in existence since the early nineteenth century but little used, became a popular way for manufacturers to encourage loyal purchasing of their own products.

Europeans and Americans, weary of the privations caused by World War II, eagerly joined in the consumer boom of the 1950s and 1960s. Back in the mid-nineteenth century the English economist and philosopher John Stuart Mill had defined true freedom as "pursuing our own good in our own way, so long as we do not attempt to deprive others of theirs, or impede their efforts to attain it."

In other words, freedom is freedom of personal choice. All that ultimately matters is that the free individual has the right to make his or her own decisions. Everything else—society, obligations to others, the common good—is secondary.

With the arrival of postwar consumerism Mill's definition of freedom has walked off the page and into the shopping mall. Here at last is the ultimate embodiment of personal liberty. I can define my very identity by the consumer choices I make. I go to the stores I choose to buy the foods, the running shoes, the jackets, the furniture that best express my chosen "lifestyle." And while I make my self-defining choices, others are free to do the same.

The supermarket shelf has also become the model for how we shop for truth and meaning. Choice is all that matters, and older, more absolute criteria of truth become obsolete. The man next to me in the canned fruit aisle might choose prunes. I choose guavas. He chooses Sikhism. I choose Christianity.[1]

For the postmodern consumer of faiths, the act of choosing is actually more important than what we choose. Religion, like prunes and guavas, is a lifestyle choice, where rules give way to preferences. I choose, therefore I am.

The View from the Couch

Watching TV is another way we assert our individualism, get targeted for commercialism and are taught the latest societal worldview. Television has become much more than something we look at. It has become a way of looking, the window through which we watch the world. When we look through a window we usually see a clear image of whatever lies behind it. But a window whose glass is tinted or distorted will affect the color or the shape of the reality we see. So it is with TV. In a culture dominated by mass media, we take the watching eye of TV for granted. We no longer ask ourselves whether our ways of looking might have an inherent bias or flaw.

TV unquestionably has a bias. It relativizes all claims to truth. Through TV the whole world is brought into our living room, including the world of religion. In the past few months I have seen programs on TV about Buddhist corpse collectors in Bangkok, a Haitian voodoo priestess living in Brooklyn, Islamic revivalists, new avenues in Christian worship, and New Agers learning sexual technique in suburban London.

Each is presented in the same dispassionate, intrigued tone. No criteria of truth or value are brought to bear. No comparison is made between rival truth claims. Even those views that are patently ridiculous are presented with apparent seriousness: the man who has been sitting in his armchair for the past ten years watching TV, the man who leaves his Christmas decorations up all year long because he loves the festive season so much. People who claim to have had postdeath meetings with Elvis are presented alongside Christians who claim to have met the risen Christ.

The medium not only conveys the message; it becomes the message. An

> **Television has become much more than something we look at. It has become a way of looking, the window through which we watch the world.**

intrinsically relativizing medium promotes the message that all truth is relative. Our media are rich in information but poor in enabling critical discernment. Any face-to-face meeting with somebody who claims to have found religious truth is met with a weary shrug of the shoulders: "I saw a man the other evening who said he was God. And last week I watched a woman who said God told her to kill her husband. And I've seen all those fanatics shouting in the streets in Iran. So what? We all find our own truth in our own way."

Jung, Nietzsche, Feuerbach

One of the thinkers who gave intellectual credibility to the idea that all religious truth is relative was the psychologist Carl Gustav Jung (1875-1961), son of a Swiss Reformed clergyman. One of Jung's key claims was that each individual has a personal unconscious as well as a collective unconscious, which is built up through history and shared by all humanity.

We tend to think of people as individuals, formed by their own culture, background and commitments. Each person's mind is seen as separate from other minds, full of its own thoughts, preferences and values. But Jung claimed that beneath the superficial differences are universal patterns or structures common to all human minds, which form the basis of our thinking and self-understanding. We are not aware of these deeper strata in normal, conscious life, but patterns or archetypes surface when the rational mind is not in control, particularly in dreams, mythologies and fantasies. Jung immersed himself in the study of ancient myths, claiming that the figures and tales found there embody not just archaic but universal motifs of human consciousness.

Archetypes stalking our unconscious minds include the *anima* (female archetype), the *animus* (male archetype), the child, the earth mother and the hero. Wholeness, or "individuation," comes from forging a healthy link between the conscious mind and the personal and collective unconscious, from accepting and respecting those hidden parts of our mind that surface in myth and dream. According to Jung this journey to psychological wholeness can best be achieved with the help of an analyst.

Talk of gods and goddesses was for Jung a way of discussing ourselves. He claimed all people have "a natural religious condition" and our psychological health depends on being in touch with this part of our own makeup. Archetypes of gods and of one's own self become indistinguishable from each other. Any idea of a transcendent, personal being beyond the self was dismissed by Jung, a lifelong occultist. The real task, he said, is to honor our inner archetypes in the search for personal wholeness, to discover the god within.

For the militantly anti-Christian German philosopher Friedrich Nietzsche (1844-1900), all religion was simply a power play of one person or group against another. For him any talk of "truth" and a claim to have access to universal or objective reality was no more than a disguise for personal advantage. All people possess an innate "will to power," to dominate others, and religion offers ample opportunities. Similarly, he claimed that morality is based on no more than a desire to preserve order in society. It too is about power games. Since the time of Nietzsche (coincidentally the son of a Lutheran clergyman) it can no longer be assumed that God is "out there," that religious people are devout seekers after truth and their morality simple obedience to the ways of God.

A third thinker whose name is less well known but whose views have had a profound influence through the works of Marx, Engels, Huxley, Freud and the novelist George Eliot is Ludwig Feuerbach (1804-1872). It was Feuerbach, and not Marx, who first described religion as opium. An explicitly anti-Christian thinker, like Nietzsche, Feuerbach decided that our talk about God is actually talk about ourselves. God is "merely the projected essence of man."

Human beings, according to this theory, have a range of natural ideals, fears and aspirations, which are projected outside ourselves and given the shapes of deities and heroes. For Feuerbach the Christian God was a personification of our own feelings of contentment and security. Religion was not a window into the beyond but a mirror in which people could see their own reflections.

Taken together, the mass media, the consumer society, and the legacy of Jung, Nietzsche and Feuerbach have had a powerful effect on the way we think about questions of truth in religion. Even if people have not heard the names of these thinkers or ever examined the social shifts of postmodernity, they will have inhaled such perspectives simply by living in society. They will almost certainly have been taught relativism as a self-evident truth in school and college.

In the name of equality and tolerance—excellent virtues in and of themselves—students have been led to believe that the only safe route toward these goals is the absolute openness of relativism. Reality becomes the reality you choose or create for yourself. No version of truth or goodness can claim a universal allegiance. Most will rarely question that religion is a quest for inner wholeness, that truth is relative, that what is right for you might not be right for me. Heresy lies not in untruth but in intolerance.

Spirituality

How then can we account for the revival of interest in religion among today's young adults if their belief in—and concern for—truth has collapsed? The answer is brief: spirituality.

Spirituality is on sale at a shopping center near you. Spirituality is fashion accessories, toiletries, wall hangings, CDs and perfumes. A fashion spread in a recent women's magazine hailed a return to "spirituality" through the use of natural, undyed fabrics. Toiletries not tested on animals are advertised as embodying "spiritual" values. Gifts made from recycled materials are billed as expressing the "spiritual" side of our nature. Jenny, twenty-one, was typical of her generation when she told me: "I never go to church, but I'm really into spirituality."

But what does it all mean? What is "spirituality" as defined by magazines and shopping malls? One of the few places I have found an attempt at a definition is in a leaflet advertising aromatherapy oils. This leaflet explains the philosophy behind the products. It describe the oils as being for "the treatment of the whole person," and the different oils are "grouped according to their effect on Body, Mind or Spirit."

But what is Spirit? The leaflet continues: "We use the term *Spirit* to convey our innermost self—the more subtle side of our nature which cannot always express itself in the turmoil of our emotions," and it suggests that the oils will be beneficial in "helping to achieve a sense of balance and composure."

Spirituality, then, means some capacity in each individual for personal depth, something akin to our emotions, but more timeless and ethereal. It is our capacity for creativity and a deep inner sense of equilibrium and well-being. It might be evoked by a CD of Gregorian chants, by shopping in an ethnic rug shop, by watching a TV program about the Amazon or by recycling household trash.

Anything can be a resource in the personal development of "spirituality" so long as it appears to foster inner depth and a sense of mystery. Whenever I go to a relig-ious retreat house I like to ask other visi-tors their reason for being there. The most frequent answer is "To deepen my personal spirituality."

> **Spirituality is on sale at a shopping center near you. Spirituality is fashion accessories, toiletries, wall hangings, CDs and perfumes.**

It is interesting to see that this definition of spirituality is becoming common even within Christian churches. I recently attended a conference run by a Christian organization and went to an optional workshop on the theme of spirituality. We were each given a sheet on which were written a number of definitions of *spirituality* and were asked to underline the one we felt best embodied its meaning. I underlined one that said something to the effect of "being empowered by the Spirit of God to live a Christian life in today's world."

The other members of the group, all of whom described them-selves as Christians, opted for definitions such as "a deep, inner feeling in myself," "my inner impulse for reaching to God," "a mystical sensation of inner harmony" or "my profound sense of the mystery in nature." Some of them ridiculed my choice for omitting words such as *inner, deep, natural* and *mystical,* which they associated with the concept of spirituality.

A close look at how the term *spirituality* is being used today, particularly by Xers, shows that spirituality is a capacity located wholly in the self. For the Xer it is simply taken for granted that spirituality is a type of self-realization and self-expression. It is almost a synonym for "the inner life."

Thomas Moore's Brand of Spirituality

We see "spirituality" in action in the work of Thomas Moore, one of today's most popular spiritual gurus, whose work is characteristic of much recent spiritual writing. His *Care of the Soul: A Guide for Cultivating Depth and Sacredness in Everyday Life*[2] spent over forty-six weeks on the *New York Times* bestseller list following its publication in 1992 and has become one of the top-selling books of spiritual guidance.

Moore is a former Roman Catholic monk who now writes and lectures on Jungian psychology. Moore's key to "cultivating depth and sacredness in everyday life" lies in the rediscovery of what he calls "soul." He admits that he cannot define what *soul* actually is, but he offers a few clues in the book. It has "to do with genuineness and depth,"[3] it is "a quality or a dimension of experiencing life and ourselves,"[4] the "infinite depth of a person and of a society, comprising all the many mysterious aspects that go together to make up our identity," and it is "the mystery we glimpse when we look deeply into ourselves."[5] At one point Moore gives up on definitions, claiming, "When we say that someone or something has soul, we know what we mean, but it is difficult to specify exactly what that meaning is."[6] He makes some intriguing assumptions, since he also tells us, "You have a soul, the tree in front of your house has a soul, but so too does the car parked under that tree."[7]

Moore is saying that soul is the capacity for being deep, for going beyond the superficial and seeing a mysterious dimension in all things. Terms such as *deep* and *depth* appear on almost every page. In other words, Moore means by *soul* what most people mean by *spirituality.* He notes that traditionally the clergy were charged with the "cure" or "care" of souls. Now, he says, "we can be the curates of our own souls, an idea that implies an inner priesthood and a personal religion."[8] It is up to each of us to develop our own spirituality.

We can do this in a variety of ways. One is by creating our own places of sacredness: boxes of memories, photo albums or personal journals.[9] But the main ways we care for our soul (and, presumably, that of our car) are by studying our own dreams and immersing ourselves in myths, rituals and religious traditions of every kind. Dreams are important because they form "a person's own mythology and imagery,"[10] offering insights into the working of our unconscious.

Jung's influence is clear. For Moore all religions and all mythologies are mirrors into our own unconscious. They reveal the archetypes inside our own brains that are inherited jointly by all humanity from primitive times. Religion and ritual do not offer a window into a reality beyond the self, but instead help the self understand its own inner workings. For example, Moore follows Jung in claiming that one of our inner archetypes is the *puer* (Latin for "boy"), or the idealistic, energetic, boyish impulse. He claims the best places to find the *puer* embodied are in Jesus (who calls himself "Son," is at odds with the establishment and so on), in the Buddha and in Shakespeare's Hamlet.[11]

So Jesus standing in the Jordan to be baptized by John is actually an archetype for our wanting to live life to the full, to "step courageously into the river of existence, instead of finding ways to remain safe, dry and unaffected."[12] And the passion of Jesus is actually an archetype of the story of love, along with the stories of Odysseus, Hamlet, and Tristan and Isolde.[13]

The picture-language of Christian tradition is no more significant than any other. We can also turn to Zen, classical Greek myths, medieval occultists, Arthurian romances, Plato and our own dreams in the search for depth. We read the Bible not to find the self-revelation of God but as a stimulus to our own "religious imagination."[14]

Moore claims that one day we will move beyond all the truth-claims of the different religions and see religion, ritual and mythology for what they really are: resources for our own self-analysis. Myths and religions are our decorated mirrors, gilded, beautiful, but ultimately only showing us ourselves: "One day I expect an 'archetypal theology' may show us the soul of religious texts from around the world."[15] What the soul needs, says Moore, is more myths, more dreams, more religion.

Deep Within

Moore is typical of a newer generation of writers on spiritual themes who are helping shape the religious consciousness of a generation. In reaction against what they see as the superficiality of contemporary culture, they stress the need for depth, for cultivating spirituality and the inner life.

••

Why should most of us find Doughboy religion half-baked? Because fictional bakers can sustain their Doughboy religion only by doing away with any criterion of truth and untruth.

••

It is an appealing vision to a generation turned on to these things but turned off by formal religious structures. "Spirituality" offers Xers the most appealing features of religion without what they see as its worst aspects. It offers inner tranquillity, a myth to live by and a sense of mystery, but without exclusive claims to truth and morality. It enables people to go deeper in their own journeys of self-realization without stepping on anyone else's toes.

But is contemporary spirituality built on a solid foundation? Does it have the capacity to change people and societies for the better?

Pillsbury Doughboy Spirituality

When I was younger my favorite TV commercial featured the Pillsbury Doughboy, a small, roly-poly figure made of bread dough. His white, doughy face beamed benevolently from the TV screen and broadened into a chuckle when a finger poked his ample stomach.

Sometimes I like to imagine a group of spiritually hungry bakers getting together to design their own religion. What, they ask, will be an authentic spirituality for breadmakers? They decide to set up small altars in their shops and homes and pay homage to the Pillsbury Doughboy. What could be more appropriate than a god who not only affirms breadmaking but actually is bread himself?

If the Doughboy is the central deity in the bakers' pantheon, then a range of other minor gods also help, including Jesus Christ (who broke bread, told his followers that he was "the bread of life," and made references to yeast). They find an array of references to breadmaking in all the myths and faiths of the world, which they put together as their scriptures under the title *Daily Bread.*

Always they are motivated by a single guiding principle: what I as a baker think will suit me and will bring me fulfillment in my breadmaking way of life.

Spirituality and Truth

Why should most of us find Doughboy religion half-baked? Because fictional bakers can sustain their Doughboy religion only by doing away with any criterion of truth and untruth. They have redefined truth to mean simply whatever suits them and their lifestyle. Just as everything in the physical world is bread to them, so everything in the spiritual world becomes bread.

Now let us imagine instead of bakers the children of the postwar consumer boom in search of religion. They are a group raised on an unparalleled choice of foods from around the world, an unprecedented range of media options, a vast choice of clothing, furnishings, reading matter and leisure pursuits. For such people the one nonnegotiable is that they stand at the center of their own universe, able to select the goods, people and experiences they desire.

Such a culture goes off in search of religion and comes up with "spirituality," their very own version of Doughboy religion. It is a religion where the self is at the center, where all the faiths and myths of history are explored in the search for happy inner experiences, where nobody and nothing impedes freedom of choice. It is spirituality as lifestyle accessory.

The spirituality of Thomas Moore and other such writers is not a genuine spirituality of wonder and astonishment. It is a Doughboy spirituality for a self-centered consumer society. For a generation reared on endless trips to the mall to try on the latest style of jeans in front of well-lit mirrors, Moore's definition of truth may be curiously comforting: "Soul knows the relativity of its claim on truth. It is always in front of a mirror, always in speculative mode, watching itself discover its developing truth, knowing that subjectivity and imagination are always in play."[16] All we can ever really know is the experience of trying on and buying whatever appears to fit comfortably.

Spirituality and Goodness
Contemporary spirituality not only assumes that all truth is relative but believes that morals are relative too: we create our own

standards of right and wrong. According to Moore, soul has its own laws, unbounded by convention and traditional ethics. Any other approach is guilty of being "moralistic."[17]

He is happy to claim that soul is "a form of consciousness with its own wisdom,"[18] that whatever wild imaginings lurk inside us are to be welcomed and celebrated: "Care of the soul means respecting its emotions and fantasies, however objectionable."[19] The only law is that we must follow the dictates of love, wherever it leads, especially if it leads beyond the confines of orthodox morality: "every love involves a transgression. Soul is to be found in the vicinity of taboo."[20]

This fundamentally self-centered ethic is seen most clearly in Moore's attitudes toward intimate relationships among people, particularly sexual relationships. In earlier chapters we discussed such intimacy as an encounter with one who is other than ourselves, that the heart of love is encounter and respect. This understanding is explicitly denied by Moore: "It may be useful to consider love less as an aspect of relationship and more an event of the soul. This is the point of view taken in ancient handbooks. There is no talk of making relationships work.... The emphasis is on what love does to the soul."[21]

If this is true, it naturally follows that love is whatever brings me personal fulfillment. It should come as no surprise to learn that eight years after Jung married his wife, Emma Rauschenbach, he took a mistress, Antonia Wolff, a relationship that lasted until his death. Although the triangular arrangement was difficult for both women, Jung was being consistent. All that ultimately mattered was his own self-defined happiness and "wholeness."

Caring for the Soul of Generation X

Any Xer with half a brain can't fail to spot the tragic irony. Generation X has inherited a world ravaged by an ideology claiming that humankind is the measure of all things. Rain forests are felled, countryside destroyed, seas polluted and poorer nations kept in poverty by a system based on personal comfort and consumer choice in the affluent West.

This is a generation that has felt all too acutely the destructive power of divorce, a generation emotionally numbed and afraid of walking the streets at night. So many long for a wonder that constantly eludes them. The damage observed by Xers in their own lives and in the world is the direct consequence of rampant relativism in truth and morals.

Certain spiritual gurus suggest that the solution lies in a spirituality of selfish individualism. But for all the use of faddish terms such as *deep, profound, inner* and *mystery,* such a spirituality is appallingly shallow. Not only does it fail to challenge the complacency of Western consumer capitalism, but it is a product of it. It doesn't challenge personal selfishness, because personal selfishness is its religious expression.

> **Consumer spirituality, far from being the answer, is simply a restatement of the problem using mystical jargon.**

Such is the religious illiteracy of our culture, that we fail to spot that such "spirituality" is no solution. We live in an age that can tell the difference between Coke and Pepsi blindfolded, but not the difference between good religion and bad religion, even with our eyes open. Consumer spirituality, far from being the answer, is simply a restatement of the problem using mystical jargon.

Are there any other way to care for our souls, or have we finally hit a dead end? The next chapter considers an alternative.

9

Hope Restored

••

The Christian ideal has not been found wanting.
It has been found difficult; and left untried.
G. K. Chesterton,
What's Wrong with the World?

*I*f theology is the study of God (from the Greek *theos*), then most contemporary spirituality is "me-ology," the art of taking my own tastes, preferences and moods and creating a customized religion just for me.

For all their talk of transcendence, eternity, the spirit and sacredness, spiritual writers such as Moore say nothing about God, an alarming omission from the perspective of historic Christianity. It means that the one central Reality that can give us bearings in the search for spirituality, identity and wonder is left out of the picture. We are left with what theologian David Wells calls the "weightlessness of God."[1]

Instead of being opened to the Mind behind the universe, we are left shut up inside the universe of our own mind. The gods of the new spirituality can inspire no wonder. They are as controllable and safe as the Pillsbury Doughboy, a projection of our own consumer preferences.

C. S. Lewis, in his classic *Miracles,* expresses well the tremor that passes down the human spine at the suspicion that perhaps God might be real, that he might be more than mere projection:

> There comes a moment when the children who have been playing at burglars hush suddenly: was that a real footstep in the hall? There comes a moment when people who have been dabbling in religion ("Man's search for God"!) suddenly draw back. "Supposing we really found Him? We never meant it to come to that!"[2]

Lewis underlines the vital Christian insight that there is such a thing as truth, and this truth is a Person. The discovery of truth comes neither from navel-gazing nor from abstract contemplation. It forces us outward, into an encounter with One other than ourselves. Moses is confronted with a burning bush, Saul is thrown from his horse and blinded, Isaiah collapses in a gibbering heap, crying, "Woe to me!" The biblical meeting with God is no comfortable spirituality. It is a terrifying and awe-inspiring encounter.

••

"It is madness to wear ladies' straw hats and velvet hats to church; we should all be wearing crash helmets. Ushers should issue life preservers and signal flares; they should lash us to our pews."

••

In the New Testament we read of Jesus' disciples, together in an upper room:

> Suddenly a sound like the blowing of a violent wind came from heaven and filled the whole house where they were sitting. They saw what seemed to be tongues of fire that separated and came to rest on each of them. All of them were filled with the Holy Spirit.[3]

I sometimes picture that as Peter and the others dashed downstairs to shout out to the world what has just happened, a distant ancestor of Jung remained upstairs and speculated on which archetype had just surfaced from the collective unconscious. But Pentecost was no archetype. It was people experiencing the raw, unleashed power of a personal God, a God beyond all their petty projections, preferences and pieties.

In Pentecost we see the true basis for Christian Spirituality, the intimate presence of the Holy Spirit of God, who along with the Father and the Son makes up the Trinity. The Christian response to spirituality (small *s*) is Spirituality (capital *S*), life charged up with the personal Spirit of God and lived out in the world.

The true God can never be tamed and domesticated. In the words of novelist Annie Dillard,

Does anyone have the foggiest idea what sort of power we so blithely evoke? Or, as I suspect, does no one believe a word of it? . . . It is madness to wear ladies' straw hats and velvet hats to church; we should all be wearing crash helmets. Ushers should issue life preservers and signal flares; they should lash us to our pews.[4]

When Christians await Sunday morning with bated breath and trembling excitement, filled with awe and wonder at coming into the presence of a living God, then perhaps the watching world will stop playing at spirituality and join us.

Identity

Today's free-for-all spirituality might feel like a victory over older, dogmatic images of God. It might feel like a liberation from the creeds and definitions that plagued theologians of earlier centuries. It soon becomes clear, however, that our victory is hollow and brief. Liberation from the "constraints" of God means liberation from the roots of human identity.

To be made in the image of God is to be made for relationship with him. God is no projection of our own ideals, values or preferences. We are not made to be alone or to find our ultimate reference point in ourselves. Over against inward-looking spirituality, Christianity insists that we can discover truth only by looking beyond ourselves to God himself, the God who is really there and who is Other. God made us for an encounter, for intimacy with himself.

The Hebrew words for worship, *hishtahawah* and *abodah,* mean "bowing before" God and "serving" him with our lives. Worship opens us outward. It is an antidote to self-centeredness.

This is why the Old Testament prophets denounced the worship of idols. It is not that in making substitute gods the people of Israel were breaking some arbitrary law, but they were being unfaithful to a relationship. Like today's "spirituality," the idols of the ancient world were the products of human introspection. But God is personal and Other, no mere projection of our own preferences. He alone is real and can bear the weight of human identity. To settle for less is to chase a reflection of our own selves.

Monotheism—fidelity to the one God—is to religion what monogamy is to human relationships. The natural human impulse, particularly in a consumer society, is to keep all options open. But the paradox is that it is only when we finally choose to shut down all other options that we discover the truth: Christian monotheism produces good worship, just as monogamy produces good sex. It is the expression of a relationship of complete trust with one who is Other than myself. Consumer spirituality, like sexual promiscuity, condemns people to perpetual frustration, because they are never able to climb out of their own heads long enough to experience the wonder of real encounter.

The Distorted Self

Faithful encounter is much harder than promiscuous self-centeredness for the simple reason that encounter, with the true God or with another person, involves a living subject and not a passive object for personal pleasure. And this opens us up to something most of us find very difficult: being shown where we are wrong. This hazard is not encountered in contemporary spirituality, because there the self is never wrong. Moore says the sign of the soulful life is that we know and accept ourselves.[5] Any sign of self-criticism is a sign of a personality that is not integrated, that has failed to honor its "shadow" or darker side.

Even our tendency toward violence is to be encouraged as an example of our own life force: "There is nothing neutral about the soul. It is the seat and the source of life. Either we respond to what the soul presents in its fantasies and desires, or we suffer from the neglect of ourselves."[6]

It seems extraordinary to me that when critics of Christianity attack it, their first target is the part of Christianity that is self-evidently true: its doctrine of sin. When I was in my early twenties I spent some time reassessing my religious faith. For a while belief in God seemed impossible and I had no choice but to see myself as an atheist. But even in my time of deepest questioning I never doubted Christianity's claim that there is something fundamentally wrong with the human heart. Malcolm Muggeridge wrote that the only part of Christianity that can be demonstrated from the morning paper is its doctrine of original sin.

Generation X marks the end point of the experiment of secular humanism. For decades society has worked on the assumption that human beings are naturally good, that our only hindrances are external, and as we pursue our personal freedom and self-realization utopia will be just around the corner. But the result of our greater freedom and our throwing off external hindrances has been unprecedented levels of divorce, unparalleled levels of addiction and a lower level of psychic well-being than any society in history. Paul Vitz, professor of psychology at New York University, asks the question that fashionable me-ology is desperate to avoid: "If people are so good, how did societies get so bad?"[7] His own conclusion is that the Christian doctrine of original sin contains the clue: there is a fundamental distortion in human nature. We need not so much self-realization as detoxification. Not individuation but salvation.

Consumer spirituality is superficially appealing, but on closer inspection its deep-seated selfishness turns out to be part of the problem. Christian Spirituality seems initially harsh and demanding, but its demands are the demands of relationship with a person, a person who tells us the truth about ourselves—even the truth we do not like to hear. It is only when we admit we are sick, as individuals and as a society, that we can begin to ask for healing.

Wonder Restored

Generation X asks, "Who am I?" The shopping mall says, "You are a consumer; buy an identity." The humanist says, "You are an individual; sort yourself out." The bestselling writer on spirituality says, "You are in need of self-realization; go deeper within."

The Xer replies, "I have bought so many identities I no longer have a clue who I am. I participate in a culture of selfishness so screwed up that I can do nothing to change my world. I have gone deeper within and found only emptiness. My inheritance is to be a person of no fixed identity in a world with no wonder."

God says, "You are a person made in my image. You are made for intimacy with me and with others, to care for my earth and develop its potential. Your inheritance is to have a stable identity in a world charged up with glory. Be reborn into wonder."

The small child looks at the universe with wide-eyed wonder. It is a world where even the oldest things become new, because the child is looking at them through her own new eyes. The journalist who has just escaped a near-fatal car crash looks at the universe with wide-eyed wonder. It is a world where even the familiar things become an astonishing gift, because that journalist looks at them with a new gratitude.

••

It is only when we admit we are sick, as individuals and as a society, that we can begin to ask for healing.

••

It is puzzling that the Christian church is so defensive and self-conscious about the one unique thing it has to offer the world: a promise of rebirth. All the consumer spirituality, all the humanist psychology, all the paganism in the world does not possess what one tacky revival tent, a wobbly organ and a preacher in a bad suit can possess: the key to wonder restored, death to selfishness and a world screwed up by human sin, rebirth into newness, intimacy with God and each other, resurgence of the vision of an earth renewed in glory. It is a hope of freshness and wonder that a whole generation longs to hear.

Appendix 1

Twelve Things to Remind You That the World Is a Wonderful Place

1. Sunny greenhouses filled with plants
2. Babies' smiles
3. Old maps of the world
4. Mexican food
5. Cold mountain streams
6. Making up after an argument
7. Rivers in the middle of cities
8. Warm fires on snowy winter nights
9. Good friends
10. Springtime
11. Seedless grapes
12. God so loved the world that he gave his one and only Son, that whoever believes in him shall not perish but have eternal life.

Appendix 2

Twelve Ways to Help Restore Lost Wonder

1. Take a toddler to the zoo.
2. Start reading poetry.
3. Give your favorite person a list of the ten things you like best about them.
4. Read a different newspaper or listen to a different radio station.
5. Try a new, daring hairstyle.
6. Fly a kite.
7. Stop watching TV for a month.
8. Surprise somebody close to you with a random act of wild generosity.
9. Read one of the four Gospels in the New Testament straight through.
10. Buy a new bike and ride it often.
11. Put on your favorite music and dance around the room (preferably with small children).
12. Take up gardening.

The Story of a Rescue
••

What is you, Scout? What is the you of you? What is the link?
Where do you begin and end? This you thing—is it an invisible
silk woven from your memories? Is it a spirit? Is it electric?
What exactly is it?

Douglas Coupland, *Life After God*

*T*onight I will sit at my children's bedside and tell them a
story. It will be a story about Jeremy, a schoolboy of indeterminate
age who lives in suburban West London. His seemingly endless
capacity for boredom leads him unwittingly into a range of
extraordinary and spine-chilling scrapes that force the listening
children under the sheets in horror, before the reassuring,
heart-warming conclusion involving food and sleep.

Telling Stories

A story can be a way of arranging the odds and ends of life into a
single narrative, the story of our own lives. It is the "big picture"
that makes sense of all the daily details and helps us find our place
in the wider scheme of things. It helps us answer questions such as:
What is this plot that my life is a part of? What is this character I
am playing? How does it relate to the other characters in the plot?

Often we carry our stories unspoken, especially if we move in circles where people do not routinely discuss purpose and meaning.

To call this big picture a story in no way prejudges whether it is true or false. *Story* here does not mean fairy tale or fantasy. Rather it is used in the sense of an account of history and life, as in "the story of the blues," "our reporter has the full story . . ." or the hymn "Tell Me the Old, Old Story." It is a description that claims to give true information about the world as it really is.

The Road and the Milestones—The Christian Story

Some worldviews, such as Buddhism, see history as a series of recurring circles. But the Christian storyline moves not in circles but straight ahead. For Christians this timeline, traced in the Bible from Genesis to Revelation, is the key to understanding the plot of history and our place in it.

Most of this book has taken a closer look at the story, or worldview, of Generation X, the dominant life story being told by young adults at the start of a new millennium. I have aimed to contrast this story with that of historic Christianity.

In Genesis we read that God created a world teeming with abundant life and declared it "very good." One part of that creation is humanity, who, not content with being dependent creatures, made a unilateral declaration of independence from their Creator. Because people were never designed to be independent from God's provision, the result was a "fall" from the perfection they had previously enjoyed.

The human world was now marred by sin; a state of rebellion, or "missing the mark," that had a ripple effect through the rest of creation. God had a choice: he could either abandon the broken earth or bring a rescue plan into effect. Because his very nature is total love and self-giving, he chose rescue.

The first stage of the rescue plan is the covenant with Israel. God chose one old man from a city near the Persian Gulf and made him a promise: that his extended family will be a prototype of what humanity can look like when restored to intimacy with God. They are to model this restored relationship to the rest of creation so that in time the whole world will be drawn in. The old man's name was Abram (soon to be changed to Abraham), his descendants the people of Israel.

••

God had a choice: he could either abandon the broken earth or bring a rescue plan into effect. Because his very nature is total love and self-giving, he chose rescue.

••

Since the effects of sin were still pervasive, part one of God's rescue plan included provisions for dealing with its effects. God gave the young nation a range of laws to enable them to live together in relative peace. And because sin poisoned the relationship between people and God, he gave them a means for dealing with it. Blood shed in sacrifices gained freedom from sin for the person offering it up. There was a substitution—animal for person.

God also littered the history of Israel with prophetic visions of a day when the perfection so briefly enjoyed in Eden (the past age) will be re-created (the age to come) and all suffering and sin of the present age will be erased. One day there really will be heaven on earth once again. And here is a crucial point: the biblical vision of eternity is not the immortality of a soul, drifting around like a loose nightshirt in an ethereal heaven. The vision is a renewed, physical earth populated by renewed, physical human beings and animals. It will be a state of what the people of Israel call *shalom:* unhindered intimacy between people, the earth and God.

In the first century A.D. came part two of God's plan, the most decisive milestone of all: God himself walked the earth as a human being. Jesus of Nazareth announced and demonstrated that the eagerly awaited age to come had started to break into the present age—in the person of Jesus himself.

The health of the future age broke in through his miracles of healing; the salvation of the future age broke in through his acts of forgiveness; the justice of the future age broke in as Jesus offered dignity to those denied it; a quality of personal relationships from the future age broke in as Jesus gathered around him a motley collection of the society of his day. Jesus, God in human flesh and prototype citizen of God's future age, began to bring the reality of the future into the present.

••

So God created man in his own image, in the image of God he created him; male and female he created them.

••

Jesus was ultimately killed. To passersby it looked like any other criminal execution by the Roman authorities, but from the perspective of God's story the death of Jesus was a final sacrifice for sin. No longer was sin a barrier between people and God. Jesus' bodily resurrection was both God's vindication of the life and death of Jesus and a foretaste that we too can one day experience resurrection from death. The story culminates in the return of Jesus to earth to bring in the promised age in all its fullness. And that great climax of history is still future.

It is only within this plot that Christians can make sense of their place in God's story. They will locate themselves somewhere around the middle of the timeline of history: able to look back to the past age, or the first part of God's rescue plan, and forward to its culmination in the age to come. Whether they are still at the start of the present age of history or near its close, only time will tell.

Christians know they are living in a time of tension, the "already but not yet" chapters of the plot, and this accounts for the mixed messages they encounter daily in life and faith. They know the reality of sin obliterated; they have started to experience the reality of the age to come in relationships with people, the world and God; but the future fullness of God's reign on the earth has not yet come. They still suffer questions and doubts, still fail to live out the love they so acutely crave and long to show others.

This is a rapid overview of the plot of the Christian story. It affirms with vigor the centrality of God. Far from a cosmic absence or impersonal force, God is real and personal—the source of all personality. In the Old Testament, when Moses asks God who he is, the answer is stark and simple. He is who he is: "God said to Moses, 'I AM WHO I AM. This is what you are to say to the Israelites: "I AM has sent me to you." ' "[1]

Similarly, individual human personality is not an illusion; it is real. We are created as truly separate selves, made to relate to others and the world around us. All of this is encapsulated in the words used by the author of Genesis to describe human nature: we are the "image of God."

The Image

The phrase is from the very first chapter of the Bible. The poet has described the origins of the earth, the skies, the oceans, plant life and animal life, and now he reaches the climax:

> Then God said, "Let us make man in our image, in our likeness, and let them rule over the fish of the sea and the birds of the air, over the livestock, over all the earth, and over all the creatures that move along the ground."
>
> So God created man in his own image,
> in the image of God he created him;

male and female he created them.[2]

It is this insight into identity that gives Christians a key to understanding their own character in the universal story.

We need to understand what's behind the idea of "image" in the ancient world. It was a common practice of rulers in the ancient Near East to leave images or statues of themselves in the provinces of their empire. These images would represent the might and majesty of the ruler to those who could not see him in person. In the same way, the coins of the ancient Near East—like our own—carried the stamped image of the monarch, another standing reminder of who was boss.

Humanity is on the earth as a visible reminder of the majesty of the invisible God. We are his representatives on earth, reminding the rest of creation of the reality of its Creator. The "image" of God is not just some dimension of our makeup, such as a capacity for reason, speech or feeling. Instead, simply by being human we are God's imagers on earth. *God* is written all the way through us. Throughout this book we have seen the profound implications this has for who we are as people, as well as how we live our lives, in three crucial areas: our relations with other people, our relations with the world around us and our spiritual journey.

At the core of our beings we have a special standing before God. We were created out of love by a God who is love and were called to love him. Our dignity and destiny can be found only in relation to God. We find purpose and identity only as we relate to him.

The way this is to be lived out at the beginning of the third millennium is summed up in the title of the old hymn "Trust and Obey." We trust God to hold us, guide us and inspire us. As we do so we throw down the gauntlet to all other philosophies and "isms" that claim to find meaning and purpose elsewhere. We are also called to obey, not a popular concept in a culture that tells us we find fulfillment only in freedom, independence, seeking truth our own way.

Here is a paradox: limits can be freeing. Our culture trains us to define liberation as freedom from all restraint. But autonomy is not liberating for people created for relationship, any more than it is liberating to "free" an animal from its natural element. We do a goldfish no favors if we pull it from its bowl, take it to see a movie and force it to eat popcorn.

Christians believe in developing a lifestyle that is obedient and pleasing to God. This does not restrict freedom, but brings freedom. We can put this in terms of a story again. A character created to live in one story is unlikely to thrive in another. If the ugly duckling remains in the plot of Hans Christian Andersen's fairy story, he discovers his true identity as a swan. But make him trip-trip-trap over a bridge ruled by an ogre and he'll soon find he's duckling à l'orange.

Here lies something of the importance of Jesus of Nazareth. Not only is he the Son of God, dying to negate sin and rising to bring new life; he also embodies in his earthly life all that humanity was created to be: in relationship to God and in obedience to God. He is the one who fully images God on earth, the new Adam, prototype of the new humanity. Our goal is to be transformed ever more into his image: "And we, who with unveiled faces all reflect the Lord's glory, are being transformed into his likeness with ever-increasing glory, which comes from the Lord, who is the Spirit."[3]

Needless to say, to be transformed into the image of Christ is not to become a first-century Jewish male woodworker. It is that we discover what we are uniquely capable of becoming as our own stories build to their climax. We can discover our true selves only in relation to God.

Notes

Chapter 1: The Awe in Ordinary
[1] G. K. Chesterton, *Autobiography*, in *Collected Works of G. K. Chesterton,* ed. George Marlin (San Francisco: Ignatius, 1988), 16:96.
[2] Quoted in M. Ward, *Gilbert Keith Chesterton* (London: Sheed & Ward, 1945), p. 45.
[3] G. K. Chesterton, "Homesick at Home," in *Collected Works of G. K. Chesterton* (San Francisco: Ignatius, 1993), 14:64.
[4] G. K. Chesterton, *Heretics*, in *Collected Works of G. K. Chesterton* (San Francisco: Ignatius, 1986), 1:55.

Chapter 2: Sex: The Lost Wonder of Intimacy
[1] Charles P. Cozic, ed., *Sexual Values* (San Diego: Greenhaven, 1995), p. 238.
[2] Ibid., p. 239.
[3] Ibid., p. 238.
[4] Glenda Riley, *Divorce: An American Tradition* (New York: Oxford University Press, 1991), p. 156.
[5] Ibid., p. 5.
[6] Ibid., p. 169.

Chapter 3: The Loss of the Sacred in the Sexual
[1] Genesis 1:31.
[2] Genesis 1:22.
[3] Genesis 1:28.
[4] Genesis 2:18.

Chapter 4: A Radical Sexual Vision
[1] Genesis 11:1-9.
[2] 1 Corinthians 13:1-7.
[3] Romans 16:25.
[4] 1 Corinthians 12:12.

[5]1 Corinthians 12:27.

[6]1 Corinthians 12:14-26.

[7]1 Corinthians 3:16.

[8]Mike Mason, *The Mystery of Marriage* (Sisters, Ore.: Multnomah, 1985), p. 27.

[9]Matthew 22:39.

[10]Mason, *The Mystery of Marriage*, p. 117.

[11]R. Michael, J. Gagnon, E. Laumann and G. Kolata, *Sex in America: A Definitive Survey* (Boston: Little, Brown, 1994).

[12]See Leland Ryken, *Worldly Saints: The Puritans As They Really Were* (Grand Rapids, Mich.: Zondervan, 1986), p. 39.

[13]David Delvin and Christine Webber, *The Big "O": Understanding and Improving Your Orgasm* (London: New English Library, 1995), p. 207.

Chapter 5: The Wonder of Intimacy Renewed

[1]1 Corinthians 6:1-20.

[2]1 Corinthians 6:16.

[3]Genesis 2:23-24.

[4]Matthew 19:4-6.

[5]Tony Campolo, *Who Switched the Price Tags? A Search for Values in a Mixed-Up World* (Waco, Tex.: Word, 1986), p. 149.

[6]Ed Wheat, *Love Life for Every Married Couple* (Grand Rapids, Mich.: Zondervan, 1980), is slightly old-fashioned in tone but contains helpful suggestions for kindling or rekindling love in a relationship.

[7]Stephen Arterburn, *Addicted to "Love"* (Glendale, Ariz.: Servant, 1996), is a good Christian analysis of unhelpful and destructive addictions to romantic and sexual fantasy.

Chapter 6: Mother Earth & the Wonder of Creation

[1]Simon Hoggart, *America: A Users Guide* (London: Collins, 1990), p. 111.

[2]David Burnett, *Dawning of the Pagan Moon* (Eastbourne, England: Monarch, 1991), p. 200.

[3]For more on this idea of ancient paganism as a kind of poetic, prophetic foreshadowing—of which Christianity is the concrete fulfillment—see G. K. Chesterton, *The Everlasting Man,* in *Collected Works of G. K. Chesterton,* ed. George Marlin and Rutler Azar (San Francisco: Ignatius, 1986), vol. 2, especially chapter 5, "Man and Mythologies"; and C. S. Lewis, *Surprised by Joy* (San Diego: Harcourt Brace, 1956), especially chapter 15, "The Beginning."

[4]1 Corinthians 15:13-15.

[5]Starhawk, *Truth or Dare: Encounters with Power, Authority and Mystery* (San Francisco: Harper & Row, 1987), pp. 4, 6.

[6]See A. B. Spencer, ed., *The Goddess Revival* (Grand Rapids, Mich.: Baker, 1995), p. 106. A good analysis of the goddess movement with a helpful Christian response.

Chapter 7: Thanking Someone for the Earth
[1] Psalm 148:7-12.
[2] Psalm 148:5-6.
[3] Psalm 104:1-2.
[4] Psalm 18:11.
[5] Isaiah 6:3.
[6] Genesis 1:26-27.
[7] Genesis 1:28.
[8] Genesis 2:15.
[9] Hebrews 13:14.

Chapter 8: God: The Wonder of Encounter
[1] See Mike Starkey, *Born to Shop* (Eastbourne, England: Monarch, 1989).
[2] Thomas Moore, *Care of the Soul* (San Francisco: HarperCollins, 1992).
[3] Ibid., p. xi.
[4] Ibid., p. 5.
[5] Ibid., p. 267.
[6] Ibid., p. 5.
[7] Ibid., p. 268.
[8] Ibid., p. xv.
[9] Ibid., p. 215.
[10] Ibid., p. 217.
[11] Ibid., p. 250.
[12] Ibid., p. 244.
[13] Ibid., p. 82.
[14] Ibid., p. 239.
[15] Ibid.
[16] Ibid., p. 246.
[17] Ibid., p. 85.
[18] Ibid., p. 86.
[19] Ibid., p. 85.
[20] Ibid.
[21] Ibid., p. 78.

Chapter 9: Hope Restored
[1] David Wells, *God in the Wasteland* (Grand Rapids, Mich.: Eerdmans, 1994), chapter 5.
[2] C. S. Lewis, *Miracles* (Glasgow: Fontana, 1960), p. 98.
[3] Acts 2:2-4.
[4] Annie Dillard, *The Annie Dillard Reader* (San Francisco: HarperCollins, 1994), p. 38.
[5] Thomas Moore, *Care of the Soul* (San Francisco: HarperCollins, 1992), p. xvii.
[6] Ibid., p. 129.
[7] Paul Vitz, *Psychology as Religion: The Cult of Self-Worship,* 2nd ed. (Grand

Rapids, Mich.: Eerdmans, 1994), p. 43.

Appendix 3: The Story of a Rescue
[1]Exodus 3:14.
[2]Genesis 1:26-27.
[3]2 Corinthians 3:18.